Great Foods without Worry

More than 90 Delicious Recipes without Wheat,
Eggs, Nuts, Dairy, Soy, and Gluten

Great Foods without Worry

More than 90 Delicious Recipes without Wheat,
Eggs, Nuts, Dairy, Soy, and Gluten

Cindy M. Moseley

ᑯᑋ
Aventine Press

Credits:
Photographs by Kim Simmons of Simmons Photography,
New Richmond, Ohio, *www.simmonsphotography.com*

Cover design by Pat Simmons of Simmons Photography,
New Richmond, Ohio

Food Stylist for cover, Linda Lawson of New Richmond, Ohio

TABLE OF CONTENTS

FORWARD

This cookbook is inspired by my children, Jonathan and Katherine. My passion has always been baking. My children's needs have allowed me to use this talent in a unique way. For years, I have been learning new ways to feed my children. My wish is that this knowledge can help others living with similar diet restrictions.

My family...

When my son, Jonathan, was seven months old, he was diagnosed with food allergies to eggs, milk, and peanuts. At 12 months old, he had an anaphylactic reaction, which skin testing later determined was caused by an accidental exposure to fish. At that time, testing also identified allergies to wheat and strawberries.

While still learning about my son's allergies, I became pregnant with my daughter, Katherine. Since my husband, Oscar, and I both have food allergies, we were told this child would have a significant chance of having food allergies as well. By 12 months old, Katie was diagnosed with allergies to eggs, peanuts, and bananas.

Even though Katie is not allergic to wheat, I made the decision to feed my children the same foods. This simplified cooking for them and ensured that my son would not be exposed to wheat accidentally, since children will inevitably share food. My son also had the chance to be the "same" as his sister. Both children would have the rest of their childhood to be "different" from other children because of their allergies, but this was at least one time in their lives when that wasn't so.

Moving on...

Feeding one's child is one of the most basic instincts as a parent. Food allergies challenged me to think very differently about how to feed my children.

Learning to bake without wheat, dairy, eggs, and nuts was no easy task. I took so many elements of baking for granted, for example, the texture that wheat gluten adds to breads and the leavening and binding that comes from eggs.

I found a few cookbooks that helped me learn about alternative flours and leavening agents. However, these cookbooks either did not avoid all the problem foods or their recipes were not ones my young children would eat. This led me to create my own recipes. Today, my children enjoy wonderful, safe treats that even their friends without food allergies love to eat!

Fortunately, my children outgrew some of their allergies. Now I want to share what I have learned with others. My hope is that this cookbook will help you create delicious foods without the ingredients you don't want.

These recipes are so easy to follow that even people who have never baked before can prepare wonderful muffins, cookies, cakes, and more that the entire family is sure the enjoy!

Cindy Moseley

Acknowledgments

I first give thanks to God for blessing me with the talent to bake and two wonderful children with food allergies so that I could realize my passion and purpose in life, helping others bake with food allergies.

To My Family: Thank you to my husband, Oscar Moseley III, for believing in me and this project. Your support means everything to me! Thank you to my children, Jonathan and Katie, who were always willing to sample my newest creations, even the disasters! Thank you to my sister, Sandra Alford; my cousin, Dr. Nsenga Johannson; and my sister-in-law, Stephanie Moseley, for helping me edit the book. Thank you to my extended family for their enthusiasm and encouragement for this project: my mother, Cheryl Lyles Ross; my grandparents, Dr. Demetrice and Marie Moore Lyles; my husband's parents, Oscar and Eula Moseley; my aunts, Peggy Lee and Cynthia Griffin; my brother, Doug Ross; and my cousin, Dr. Cherice Greene.

Thank you to the Food Allergy Awareness, Support & Training, Inc. (FAAST) of Cincinnati for their financial contribution to this project. And thank you to Jennifer Redmond, founder of FAAST, for editing this book. Jennifer, your support was invaluable!

Thank you to my friend, Candy Cavalier, for editing this book.

Thank you to Jennifer Black, Dr. Charlene Brown, Gia Borgerson, Dr. Joan Cook-Mills, Amie Meyer, Lori Patton, and Christy Stergiopoulas for tasting and testing recipes for this book.

Thank you to Kim Simmons and Pat Simmons of Simmons Photography for photographing and designing the cover to this book. And thank you to Linda Lawson, food stylist for the photographs on the cover.

Thank you to Bob's Red Mill, Authentic Foods™ , and Ener-G Foods™ for donating products for this project.

Thank you to Evelyn M. and her son for giving me the opportunity to see how much I love helping people learn to bake with food allergies.

Thank you to author Carol Fenster of Savory Palate, who provided ideas, feedback, and suggestions for this project.

CHAPTER 1
GETTING STARTED

Why Some Foods Must Be Avoided
Baking without Common Ingredients
Glossary of Ingredients
Basic Tools
Staple Ingredients
Baking Tips
About This Book
Final Thoughts

WHY SOME FOODS MUST BE AVOIDED

FOOD ALLERGIES

Food allergies are an abnormal immune system response to a food protein. The immune system mistakenly interprets a food as harmful and triggers numerous whole-body reactions such as hives; swelling of the lips, tongue or throat; itchy rash; difficulty breathing; vomiting; and diarrhea. An allergic reaction usually occurs within minutes to a couple of hours after ingesting the food. The most severe reaction, anaphylaxis, may cause a drop in blood pressure, unconsciousness, or death.

According to the Food Allergy & Anaphylaxis Network, an estimated 6 to 7 million Americans (2 to 2.5% of the population) suffer from food allergies. Within that population, about 1% of adults and 7% of children are affected. While any food can potentially trigger an allergic response, eight foods are responsible for 90% of all food allergies. Those foods are peanuts, tree nuts, fish, shellfish, eggs, milk, wheat, and soy.

Today, there is no cure for food allergies. The only treatment is strict avoidance of the offending food. This requires careful reading of labels and identifying any risks of cross-contact to ensure that products are safe. Eliminating one of the eight common allergens still leaves some options for purchasing prepared or packaged foods. However when several foods must be avoided, particularly wheat and soy, baking at home is sometimes the only safe option.

CELIAC DISEASE

Celiac disease, or gluten intolerance, is also an abnormal immune system response, similar to food allergies. With celiac disease, the immune system reacts to foods containing a protein called gluten, which is present in wheat, barley, rye, oats, spelt, triticale, and kamut. Reactions include diarrhea, vomiting, bloating, gas, and abdominal pain. The disease also interferes with proper nutrient absorption. Consequently, symptoms of fatigue, weight loss, anemia, and osteoporosis can occur. Left untreated, there is a much greater risk of gastrointestinal cancer.

According to the Celiac Sprue Association, an estimated 1 in 133 Americans may be affected with celiac disease. There is no cure for celiac disease. Only strict avoidance of all grains containing gluten will halt the progressive damage to the body. Buying prepared or packaged foods can be difficult when avoiding gluten. Derivations of wheat and other glutens are found in countless products, often hidden within names such as "modified food starch." Baking foods at home is often the best alternative to ensure that all gluten is avoided.

VEGETARIAN / VEGAN DIETS

This cookbook is also suitable for people choosing vegetarian or vegan diets. Both vegetarians and vegans avoid all meat, poultry, and fish, while vegans also avoid all animal by-products, including milk (dairy) products, eggs, and gelatin. All of the recipes in this cookbook are free of eggs and dairy, and Agar, a seaweed product, can be substituted for gelatin. Additionally, vegetarian products like tofu can be used in the recipes that use meat, provided soy is appropriate for your diet.

BAKING WITHOUT COMMON INGREDIENTS

WHEAT

An allergy to wheat can be very difficult, because wheat is found in so many commercially prepared foods. And baking without wheat can be challenging since wheat has different functions, such as providing structure, texture, and flavor. No single flour completely mimics the characteristics of wheat, so a combination of flours is required to achieve the same effect.

In this book, the primary flours of choice are brown rice flour, tapioca flour, and potato starch. Oat flour is also used because of its nutritional content and its flavor. To bake without gluten, substitute oat flour with sorghum, quinoa, or soy flour (for those not allergic to soy). The flavor will only be slightly altered.

EGG

Baking without eggs can be almost as challenging as baking without wheat. Eggs provide three important functions in baking: leavening, binding, and adding moisture. Like wheat, there is no single complete substitute. Instead, there are substitutes for each of the functions.

For leavening, use baking powder, baking soda, yeast, and Egg Replacer from Ener-G Foods™. For binding, xanthan gum, guar gum, pureed fruit, gelatin, and a gel derived from flax meal work well. Moisture can be added from pureed fruits like applesauce, bananas, and apricots. Additional liquids and oil can also be added to improve moisture.

MILK

Milk is relatively easy to substitute in baking. Rice milk was the milk used for all the recipes in this book. The viscosity is similar to cow's milk, and the difference in taste is minimal in baked goods. If soy milk is used, extra liquid (water or more soy milk) may be required since soy milk is thicker than rice or cow's milk, so there is less liquid for the same volume. Be sure that any alternative milk, whether soy or rice, does not contain unwanted ingredients such as gluten from barley malt extract, or milk protein from casein.

Substituting for butter or margarine is a bit trickier. If you are avoiding either soy or dairy, there are several choices available. If you must avoid both soy and dairy, read labels carefully. These recipes were tested with a margarine that contains soy oil and soy lecithin. According to the Food Allergy & Anaphylaxis Network, both soy ingredients in this margarine are safe for most soy-allergic individuals. Consult your personal healthcare provider to ensure both ingredients are appropriate for your allergy.

SOY

Baking without soy is relatively simple with the exception of margarines, as mentioned above. Canola oil was used in all recipes requiring oil. Canola oil is readily available in most grocery stores and at a comparable price to vegetable oil (soybean oil). If soy oil is appropriate for your diet, then feel free to use it in recipes requiring oil.

Buying prepared foods, on the other hand, is quite a challenge. Soy and its by-products are quite widespread in commercial products. Diligent label-reading and verification with manufacturers is the only way to ensure a product is safe. As with wheat-free diets, soy-free diets often require preparing the majority of foods at home.

PEANUTS and TREE NUTS

Peanuts and tree nuts are quite easily avoided in recipes. However, avoiding them in prepared foods is a little more difficult. Some treats are prepared with safe ingredients for allergic individuals, but unfortunately the preparation of those foods is unsafe due to the risk of cross-contamination. This will be indicated on ingredient labels by phrases such as "may contain..." or "produced on same equipment as..." I know from experience with my own children that "a little is a lot" with peanut allergies, so even a small amounts of cross-contact is enough to make a food unsafe.

Having nut allergies means preparing most desserts at home, so there are three chapters in the book just for cookies, cakes and other desserts.

GLUTEN

Gluten is another ingredient that is found in the most unlikely products. Because the recipes in this book use only simple ingredients, gluten can be omitted by carefully reading labels and verifying with manufacturers. For example, a gluten-free version of baking powder should be chosen. In the case of oats and oat flour, simply follow the substitutions listed for each recipe to achieve a gluten-free recipe.

GLOSSARY OF INGREDIENTS

Agar – derived from seaweed; comes in powder or flakes; can substitute for gelatin for people choosing vegan diets.

Allspice – (also called Jamaican pepper) derived from the dried berries of a Jamaican evergreen tree; looks like peppercorns; a fragrant, sweet-tasting spice that is great for muffins and desserts, as well as savory dishes.

Amaranth – gluten-free flour derived from the seeds of broadleaf plants related to spinach, beets, and quinoa; refrigerate or freeze to prevent rancidity (due to high fat content).

Applesauce – adds moisture and improves binding in egg-free recipes; choose unsweetened versions.

Arrowroot – gluten-free flour derived from the roots of various plants; fine, white powder that is an excellent thickener; can be used in place of tapioca starch.

Ascorbic acid (Vitamin C) – comes in crystals or powder; adds an acidic component to recipes to improve the leavening action of yeast; choose unbuffered version.

Baking powder – leavening agent made from a combination of baking soda and starches (usually corn starch and cream of tartar); ensure gluten-free if needed; if reducing sodium in diet, sodium-free baking powder is available (made from potassium bicarbonate); choose double-acting baking powder, which means it bubbles when wet and again when heated; check expiration date to ensure freshness.

Baking soda – leavening agent; chemical name is sodium bicarbonate; derived from naturally occurring sodium carbonate (soda ash); four times as potent as baking powder; used in recipes with acidic components such as molasses, brown sugar, cocoa, and citrus juices.

Barley flour – gluten-containing flour derived from barley grains; does not contain as much gluten as wheat, so it will not rise as well; good in pie crusts, breads, and crackers.

Barley flour, malted – gluten-containing flour derived from germinated barley grains; slightly sweet flour that helps baked goods stay fresh longer.

Barley malt extract – gluten-containing powder derived from the evaporated concentrate of barley malt; natural sweetener that helps baked goods stay fresh longer.

Brown rice flour – gluten-free flour derived from rice grains; good source of fiber and nutrients; refrigerate to prolong life.

Brown sugar – white sugar with added molasses; adds chewy texture to cookies.

Canola – derived from the Canadian rape seed; available as pure canola oil as well as blended with soy and other oils; also available in a margarine spread; read labels carefully because canola margarine may contain dairy and/or soy.

Carob flour – gluten-free flour derived from the carob plant, a legume; naturally sweet; can be used instead of cocoa powder.

Cassava flour – gluten-free flour derived from the same plants as tapioca starch; courser than tapioca starch.

Cheese – dairy-free cheeses are available made from soy and rice; read labels carefully since some soy-free cheeses contain dairy and dairy-free cheeses contain soy.

Chickpea flour – see Garbanzo bean flour.

Chocolate – gluten-free; derived from cacao trees; most commercially prepared chocolates may be cross-contaminated with nuts. These recipes used cocoa and chocolate chips from the Vermont Nut Free Chocolate Company (address can be found in Chapter 12).

Cinnamon – derived from the inner bark of evergreen trees; sweet, fragrant spice that adds a wonderful flavor to muffins, cookies, and other desserts.

Cinnamon sugar – sprinkle over muffins and crackers for extra flavor and color; mix 1/2 cup sugar and 1 teaspoon cinnamon; store in shaker for easy use.

Cloves – derived from the flower buds of clove trees; very fragrant; use small amounts in baked goods to add distinct flavor.

Cocoa – see Chocolate.

Cooking spray – prevents baked goods from sticking to pans; can be made at home by using a non-aerosol bottle and pump filled with cooking oil like canola or olive oil. Commercial aerosol versions contain soy lecithin, so check with healthcare provider to ensure this is appropriate for your diet (if avoiding soy).

Corn flour – gluten-free flour derived from corn; adds distinct corn flavor to breads and batters; makes great corn bread.

Corn meal – gluten-free meal derived from corn; comes in varying degrees of coarseness; choose medium or fine-grain meal for baking; adds a crunchy texture to fried batters.

Corn starch – gluten-free flour derived from corn; excellent thickener that can substitute for tapioca starch.

Cream of Tartar – chemical name is tartrate salt; white powder derived from the crystalline acid deposited on the inside of wine barrels; serves as the acidic component to aid the leavening action of baking soda; found with spices in stores; helps stabilize (hold together) egg-free breads and muffins.

Dough Enhancer™ -- gluten-free product made by Authentic Foods™ (address can be found in Chapter 12); a combination of lecithin, ascorbic acid, tapioca flour, and ginger; improves the texture, flavor, and shelf life of breads; also improves the leavening action of yeast; check with healthcare provider to ensure this is appropriate for your diet (if avoiding soy).

Egg Replacer™ – gluten-free white powder made by Ener-G Foods™ (address can be found in Chapter 12); a combination of leavening agents and starches; a good substitute for the leavening action of eggs; recipes will still require additional ingredients for binding and moisture.

Extracts or flavorings – made from flavor (for example, vanilla, lemon, orange) and alcohol; choose gluten-free if required.

Fava bean flour – gluten-free flour derived from the fava bean, a legume; somewhat strong flavor, high in protein and other nutrients; often found in combination with garbanzo bean flour.

Flax – gluten-free; sold as whole flax seed or ground flax meal (dark or golden); high in omega-3 fatty acids; when boiled in water, flax produces a gel (resembling egg whites) that adds moisture and binding to baked goods. Due to its high fat content, flax has a very short shelf life, so it needs to be kept refrigerated or frozen to prevent rancidity.

Flours:
>**Grain flours containing gluten** – wheat, barley, rye, oat, spelt, triticale
>**Grain flours without gluten** – rice, corn, milo, sorghum, millet, teff
>**Legume flours** –chickpea (or garbanzo bean), fava, carob, soy
>**Non-grain/plant flours** – arrowroot, amaranth, quinoa
>**Tuber flours** – tapioca, cassava, white potato, sweet potato, yam, malanga
>**Nut flours** – almond, peanut, hazelnut
>*Flours avoided in this book: wheat, rye, spelt, triticale, all nut flours*

Fruit – apples, pears, and berries are great for pies and cobblers; citrus fruits (oranges and lemons) are great for accent flavors in desserts, muffins, and cakes. In most cases, frozen fruits are just as good as fresh fruits, if not better, because frozen fruits can be stored longer, and fruits not in season can be available year round. If using frozen, thaw first, unless the recipe states otherwise.

Fruit purees – applesauce, mashed bananas, pureed prunes, and pureed apricots all can be used as binders and can replace some of the fat added by oil; each fruit imparts its own flavor, color, and texture. Applesauce is used in this book because of its mild flavor.

Garbanzo bean flour (chickpea) – gluten-free flour derived from garbanzo beans (chickpeas), a legume; somewhat strong, nutty flavor, high in protein and other nutrients; often found in combination with fava bean flour.

Garbanzo/Fava – gluten-free flour; packaged as a combination of garbanzo and fava bean flour.

Gelatin – derived from animal by-products; serves as a binder in egg-free recipes; choose unflavored gelatin.

Ginger – derived from ginger roots; slightly sweet and spicy flavor that is great for both sweet and savory dishes.

Guar gum – gluten-free powder derived from seaweed; a substitute for xanthan gum; provides structure in gluten-free baking by trapping the gas produced by yeast, baking soda, or baking powder so the baked goods will rise.

Honey – a natural sweetener; imparts a distinct flavor to baked goods; not safe for very young children due to risk of botulism.

Jellies/Jams – used in muffins and cookies in this cookbook; be sure to read labels to ensure all ingredients are safe.

Leavening – Carbon dioxide (a gas) is released when baking soda (a base) is heated with water and an acidic ingredient (for examples, cream of tartar, vinegar, citric acid). The gas bubbles are trapped in the dough, forming air pockets. This makes the dough rise (increase in volume) and creates lightness and texture in breads.

Maple syrup – derived from the boiled down sap of the sugar maple tree; choose pure maple syrup since some types of syrup may contain dairy as well as preservatives and artificial flavors.

Margarine – read labels carefully since some dairy-free versions contain soy and soy-free versions contain dairy; some brands may not be suitable for baking due to high water content; stick versions work the best.

Masa – derived from corn milled with lime; make sure it does not contain wheat or gluten; great for corn tortillas.

Milk – derived from cows, goats, rice grains, soybeans, or nuts; each has its own flavor, nutritional profile, texture, and thickness; choose enriched versions for added nutrients; additional milk may be required if using soy milk due to thickness; be sure that any milk chosen does not have unwanted ingredients like gluten or casein.

Millet flour – gluten-free flour derived from millet grains; adds nutrition to baked goods.

Molasses – derived from cane sugar; strong flavor, used as sweetener in baking; also good in meat marinades.

Nutmeg – derived from the inner seed kernel of nutmeg trees; sweet fragrant spice; use small amounts in baked goods to add distinct flavor.

Oat flour – gluten-containing flour derived from oat grains; adds flavor and texture to wheat-free muffins; can be gritty in large amounts so it is best blended with other flours. For gluten-free recipes, sorghum flour makes an excellent substitution.

Oats – contains gluten; whole oat grain comes in various forms: rolled old fashion (larger pieces), rolled quick cooking (smaller oats); rolled instant ("precooked"), steel cut (uniform size and shape), and thick cut. Cooking times increase with the size of oats; choose rolled quick cooking oats for baking.

Oil – canola and olive oil are used in this book. In muffins, melted butter or margarine can be used in place of oil.

Pasta – wheat-free packaged pastas are made from rice or from a blend of quinoa and corn flour; follow cooking directions exactly since these pastas will overcook quickly.

Potato flour – gluten-free flour derived from whole potatoes, including skins; dense flour; use only in small amounts to add bulk to baked goods.

Potato starch – gluten-free flour derived from the starch of potatoes; fine, white powder with mild flavor that adds light, airy texture to wheat-free baking.

Quinoa flour – gluten-free flour derived from quinoa grains; nutritious flour with a distinct, nutty flavor; best blended with other flours.

Rice flours – gluten-free flours all derived from rice grains; a staple flour in wheat-free baking; can be gritty so it is best blended with lighter flours like potato starch and tapioca starch.

     Brown rice – rice kernel with outer husk (bran) removed; has more flavor than white rice;

     Rice bran –outer husk of rice kernel, the portion which has been removed to make brown rice;

     White rice – rice kernel stripped of most of its nutrients; bland flavor;

     Rice polish – the portion of brown rice kernel which has been removed to make white rice.

Rice milk – derived from rice grains; read labels carefully to be sure rice milk is free of gluten, dairy, or soy, as needed; choose enriched original versions for added nutrients.

Rye flour – gluten-containing flour derived from rye grains; dark flour with strong flavor; has similar properties to wheat in baking; not used in this book.

Safflower oil – derived from safflower plants; high in monounsaturated fats and low in saturated fats.

Salt – table salt has fine crystals that dissolve easily; kosher salt is coarser than table salt and works well for topping crackers; kosher salt does not dissolve well, so it is not suitable for baking; sea salt has even larger crystals which are best for topping pretzels and savory breads.

Shortening – most shortening is made from a blend of soy oil and other oils (usually cottonseed); Spectrum™ makes a 100% palm oil, which is a good substitute for soy oil-based shortening.

Sorghum flour – gluten-free flour derived from grains similar to millet; nutritious flour with slightly sweet flavor; can be gritty in large amounts so blend with other flours.

Soy – gluten-free flour derived from soybeans; a legume. Soy flour can be substituted for sorghum or oat flour if it is appropriate for your diet.

Spices – sweet spices include cinnamon, allspice, nutmeg, and ginger; savory spices include salt, pepper, garlic, onion, paprika, and turmeric; read labels to ensure there are no added ingredients.

Sugar – granulated white sugar is made from cane or beet sugar; brown sugar is made from white sugar with molasses; confectioners' sugar (powdered sugar) is highly refined sugar with added cornstarch.

Sweet rice flour (or glutinous rice flour) – gluten-free flour derived from short-grain rice or "sushi rice;" sticky and slightly sweet; great for cookies and other wheat-free desserts. Use only small amounts because it can cause a heavy, gritty end product.

Tapioca flour (or starch) – gluten-free flour derived from cassava plants; fine, white powder that adds light, airy texture to wheat-free baking.

Teff flour – gluten-free flour derived from teff grains; ancient African cereal grain with distinct flavor and dark color; adds nutrition to baked goods.

Triticale – gluten-containing flour derived from grains related to wheat and rye; not suitable for wheat-allergic individuals; not used in this book.

Vanilla – derived from the pods of orchid plants; vanilla extract is vanilla beans blended with alcohol, which may contain gluten, so check with manufacturer; vanilla powder is the ground whole vanilla beans. Because there is no alcohol, vanilla powder does not evaporate when heated, so one quarter to one half as much is needed in recipes.

Vinegar – can come from corn grains, apple cider, wine, or rice wine; adds acidity to dough to aid in leavening. Be sure vinegar is gluten-free, if needed.

Vitamin C – see Ascorbic acid.

Yeast – leavening agent in breads; check expiration date to ensure fresh yeast.

Yogurt –dairy-free versions are usually made from soy and soy-free versions that are made from rice may contain dairy. Read labels carefully.

Xanthan gum – gluten-free powder derived from a microorganism that is grown in a corn sugar; provides structure in gluten-free baking by trapping the gas produced by yeast, baking soda, or baking powder so baked goods will rise.

Zest – the outermost peel of citric fruits (lemons, oranges, limes); use zester, wood rasp, or knife to remove the peel, being careful not to cut into the bitter, white part; chop finely before adding to recipes.

BASIC TOOLS NEEDED

- Sturdy measuring cups: 1/8, 1/4, 1/3, 1/2, and 1 cup
- Sturdy measuring spoons: 1/8, 1/4, 1/2, 1 teaspoon, and 1 tablespoon
- Liquid measuring glass in 1-cup size
- Good non-stick skillet and non-stick spatulas
- Mixing bowls
- Whisks
- Pastry cutter
- Pastry scraper
- Rolling pin or pizza roller
- 1" melon baller
- Biscuit cutter
- Zester
- Muffin pan (12-count)
- Mini loaf pans (These recipes used 3 ½" by 2½" pans.)
- 6" and 8" round cake pans
- Baking sheets, at least two
- Parchment paper
- Wax paper
- Cooking thermometer
- Blender
- Electric mixer

STAPLE INGREDIENTS

These are the basic ingredients found in most of the recipes so keep them readily available for baking.

Brown rice flour
Tapioca flour
Potato starch
Sweet white rice flour
Other flours of choice (sorghum, oat, barley, soy, quinoa, millet)
Xanthan gum
Egg Replacer™
Baking powder
Baking soda
Cream of tartar
Salt
Margarine
Shortening (soy oil or palm oil)
Oil (canola or soy oil)
Milk (rice, soy, or cow)
Applesauce
Sugars – white, brown, confectioners'
Spices – cinnamon, nutmeg, allspice, ginger
Extracts – vanilla, lemon

BAKING TIPS

• Read flour labels and follow manufacturer's storage recommendation to prolong shelf life.
• Measure flours at room temperature.
• Quick breads and muffins do not require a lot of mixing. Stir with a spoon (not a whisk) just until moistened.
• Check expiration date to ensure freshness of baking powder and yeast.
• Always preheat the oven.
• If using frozen fruit, do not thaw first, unless otherwise indicated.
• Do not sift non-wheat flours. They often will not flow through the mesh of sifters.
• Since compressed flours can overfill measuring cups, aerate flours

before measuring by gently squeezing the bag, or stirring if in a container.

- Measure using the "scoop and swipe" method. Scoop the flour with a dry measuring cup and swipe off the excess with the flat side of a knife. (Spooning the flour into the measuring cup can compresses the flour and results in overfilling.)
- Mix dry ingredients thoroughly with a whisk before adding liquids. Some flours are very light and will not evenly distribute unless the dry ingredients are thoroughly mixed before adding the liquid.
- Always use a liquid measuring glass for liquids and dry measuring cups for flours. They are not interchangeable.
- Read the level of liquids in a measuring glass at eye level.
- Parchment paper helps the bottoms of cookies and cakes brown evenly and release from pans easily. If parchment paper is not available and the recipe calls for greased paper, then grease the pan; otherwise bake on the pan directly. For cakes only, wax paper can be used to help the cake release from the pan; however, the bottom will not brown as well.
- Follow recipes and substitutions exactly, particularly for leavening ingredients. Slight changes can dramatically alter the outcome.
- Freeze muffins and quick breads if not consumed immediately. Since these recipes use no preservatives, they tend to dry out quickly, especially in the refrigerator.
- If there is a recipe you make often, measure out multiple batches of the dry ingredients. Store each batch in labeled, zippered bags for quick use. Exception: If the recipe calls for creaming margarine with sugar, omit the sugar from dry ingredients for storage.

ABOUT THIS BOOK

The recipes in this book are all free of wheat, eggs, and nuts. Soy, dairy, and gluten can either be added to or omitted from almost every recipe to customize it to your needs. Simply follow the substitutions for each recipe. Also, each of the flours has its own flavor, texture, color, and nutritional properties. Try varying the flours according to your own personal preference.

FINAL THOUGHTS

Baking without these common foods requires more ingredients than otherwise required in typical recipes to achieve the same affect. And some of these ingredients are more expensive than their common counterparts. But the end result will be worth the extra effort and expense...delicious muffins, cookies, crackers, and desserts that are safe and healthy for your entire family.

Good luck and have fun learning wonderful, new ways to prepare your favorite foods. My wish for you and your family is health, happiness, and *Great Foods without Worry!*

COMMENTS

CHAPTER 2
PANCAKES and WAFFLES

Gluten-free Rice Pancakes
Apple Cinnamon Pancakes
Banana Pancakes
Blueberry Pancakes
Chocolate Chip Pancakes
Oatmeal Pancakes
Waffles

These pancake recipes are quick and easy to prepare and most are simple variations on the same recipe, so you can easily satisfy the tastes of everyone at the same time!

GLUTEN-FREE RICE PANCAKES

1/2 cup brown rice flour
1/2 cup tapioca flour
2 tablespoons potato starch
1/4 teaspoon xanthan gum
1 tablespoon Egg Replacer™
4 teaspoons baking powder
1/4 teaspoon salt
1/3 cup sugar
2 tablespoons oil (canola or soy)
1 teaspoon vanilla extract
1 1/3 cup water

Preheat a non-stick skillet over medium heat. Combine dry ingredients in a bowl. Pour water, vanilla, and oil into a blender, and then add dry ingredients. Blend until frothy. If mixing by hand, whisk vigorously until frothy.

Pour silver-dollar sized pancakes onto lightly oiled skillet. Cook until golden brown on both sides.

Makes 16 pancakes.

Tip: To save some time and effort, mix multiple batches of dry ingredients and store in individual bags for quick use later. Be sure to label each bag with the date to ensure maximum freshness. Store the bags in a cool, dry place or in the refrigerator for extended life.

APPLE CINNAMON PANCAKES

Gluten-free Rice Pancake Recipe
1/2 cup brown rice flour
1/2 cup tapioca flour
2 tablespoons potato starch
1/4 teaspoon xanthan gum
1 tablespoon Egg Replacer™
4 teaspoons baking powder
1/4 teaspoon salt
1/3 cup sugar
2 tablespoons oil (canola or soy)
1 teaspoon vanilla extract
1 1/3 cup water
plus
1/2 cup dried diced apples
1 teaspoon cinnamon

To re-hydrate the dried apples, soak them in water for a few seconds and drain well on a paper towel.

Preheat a non-stick skillet over medium heat. Combine dry ingredients in a bowl. Pour water, vanilla, and oil into a blender, and then add dry ingredients. Blend until frothy. If mixing by hand, whisk vigorously until frothy.

Pour silver-dollar sized pancakes onto lightly oiled skillet. Immediately place apples inside each pancake. Cook until golden brown on both sides.

Makes 16 pancakes.

Note: Do not use fresh apples because the higher water content will make pancakes mushy.

BANANA PANCAKES

Gluten-free Rice Pancake Recipe
1/2 cup brown rice flour
1/2 cup tapioca flour
2 tablespoons potato starch
1/4 teaspoon xanthan gum
1 tablespoon Egg Replacer™
4 teaspoons baking powder
1/4 teaspoon salt
1/3 cup sugar
2 tablespoons oil (canola or soy)
1 teaspoon vanilla extract
1 1/3 cup water
plus
1/2 cup banana, smashed with a fork

Preheat a non-stick skillet over medium heat. Combine dry ingredients in a bowl. Pour water, vanilla, and oil into a blender, and then add dry ingredients. Blend until frothy. If mixing by hand, whisk vigorously until frothy.

Pour silver-dollar sized pancakes onto lightly oiled skillet. Immediately place pieces of smashed bananas inside each pancake. Cook until golden brown on both sides.

Makes 16 pancakes.

BLUEBERRY PANCAKES

Gluten-free Rice Pancake Recipe
1/2 cup brown rice flour
1/2 cup tapioca flour
2 tablespoons potato starch
1/4 teaspoon xanthan gum
1 tablespoon Egg Replacer™
4 teaspoons baking powder
1/4 teaspoon salt
1/3 cup sugar
2 tablespoons oil (canola or soy)
1 teaspoon vanilla extract
1 1/3 cup water
plus
1/2 cup blueberries, fresh or frozen, thawed, and drained

Preheat a non-stick skillet over medium heat. Combine dry ingredients in a bowl. Pour water, vanilla, and oil into a blender, and then add dry ingredients. Blend until frothy. If mixing by hand, whisk vigorously until frothy.

Pour silver-dollar sized pancakes onto lightly oiled skillet. Immediately place 5 to 6 well-drained blueberries inside each pancake. Cook until golden brown on both sides.

Makes 16 pancakes.

Note: Placing blueberries on top of cooking pancakes prevents purple streaks and keeps the tops of the pancakes evenly browned.

CHOCOLATE CHIP PANCAKES

Gluten-free Rice Pancake Recipe
1/2 cup brown rice flour
1/2 cup tapioca flour
2 tablespoons potato starch
1/4 teaspoon xanthan gum
1 tablespoon Egg Replacer™
4 teaspoons baking powder
1/4 teaspoon salt
1/3 cup sugar
2 tablespoons oil (canola or soy)
1 teaspoon vanilla extract
1 1/3 cup water
plus
1/2 cup semi-sweet chocolate chips

Preheat a non-stick skillet over medium heat. Combine dry ingredients in a bowl. Pour water, vanilla, and oil into a blender, and then add dry ingredients. Blend until frothy. If mixing by hand, whisk vigorously until frothy.

Pour silver-dollar sized pancakes onto lightly oiled skillet. Immediately place chocolate chips inside each pancake. Cook until golden brown on both sides.

Makes 16 pancakes.

Note: Placing chocolate chips on top of cooking pancakes prevents the chocolate chips from melting while the first side is cooking. Some melted chocolate may remain on the skillet after the pancakes are removed. Simply wipe off with damp paper towel, oil the skillet again, and continue cooking the remaining pancakes.

OATMEAL PANCAKES

This recipe is not gluten-free.

1/2 cup brown rice flour
1/2 cup oat flour
1/2 teaspoon tapioca flour
2 tablespoons potato starch
2 tablespoons oats
1/4 teaspoon xanthan gum
1 tablespoon Egg Replacer™
1 tablespoon + 2 teaspoons baking powder
1 teaspoon cinnamon
1/4 teaspoon salt
1/2 cup sugar
2 tablespoons oil (canola or soy)
1 teaspoon vanilla extract
2 cups water or milk (rice, soy, or cow)

Preheat a non-stick skillet over medium heat. Combine dry ingredients in a bowl. Pour water or milk, vanilla, and oil into a blender, and then add dry ingredients. Blend until frothy. If mixing by hand, whisk vigorously to make frothy.

Pour silver-dollar sized pancakes onto lightly oiled skillet. Cook until golden brown on both sides.

Makes 16 pancakes.

WAFFLES

1 cup brown rice flour
1/2 cup potato starch
1/4 cup tapioca starch
1/4 cup oat flour or sorghum flour (for gluten-free)
1/8 cup sweet white rice flour
1 teaspoon xanthan gum
2 tablespoons Egg Replacer™
1 tablespoon baking powder
1/4 teaspoon salt
1 teaspoon cinnamon
1/4 cup sugar
1/2 cup softened margarine or oil
2 cups milk (rice, soy, or cow)

Preheat waffle iron. Combine dry ingredients in a bowl and set aside.

If using margarine, in another bowl, use electric mixer to cream margarine. Alternate adding milk with dry ingredients and mix well.

If using oil, add milk and oil to dry ingredients all at once and mix well.

Pour into greased preheated waffle iron and cook according to waffle iron directions.

COMMENTS

CHAPTER 3
MUFFINS and QUICK BREADS

Basic Muffins
Jelly-filled Muffins
Applesauce Spice Muffins
Banana Muffins
Blueberry Lemon Muffins
Carrot Muffins
Cranberry Orange Muffins
Oatmeal Cinnamon Muffins
Sweet Potato Muffins
Pumpkin Muffins
Double Chocolate Chip Muffins
Corn Meal Muffins
Cranberry Orange Bread
Zucchini Bread

Muffins are a favorite in my family, because they are easy to make and my children love them. I always bake multiple batches and freeze them to save some time and effort. The first eight recipes are all variations on the same recipe, so you can make "generic" mixes ahead of time and decide later how to finish them.

BASIC MUFFINS

1 cup brown rice flour
1/2 cup potato starch
1/4 cup tapioca flour
1/4 cup oat flour or sorghum flour (for gluten-free)
1/2 teaspoon xanthan gum
1 tablespoon Egg Replacer™
1 teaspoon baking powder
3/4 teaspoon baking soda
1/2 teaspoon cream of tartar
1/4 teaspoon salt
2/3 cup sugar
1/3 cup oil (canola or soy)
1 teaspoon vanilla extract
1/2 cup milk (rice, soy, or cow)
1/2 cup applesauce

Preheat oven to 375° F. Grease 12 muffin cups or line with baking paper.

Mix all dry ingredients thoroughly in a bowl. Make a well in the center of the dry ingredients, and then add applesauce, milk, vanilla, and oil into the well. Stir just until mixed. Pour into prepared muffin pan. Sprinkle each muffin with sugar and bake for 15 minutes or until lightly browned.

JELLY-FILLED MUFFINS

Prepare muffin batter for Basic Muffins. Fill muffin cups halfway and add 1/2 teaspoon of jelly to the center of each muffin. Then cover with remaining batter. Sprinkle each muffin with sugar and bake as directed.

APPLESAUCE SPICE MUFFINS

Basic Muffin Recipe
1 cup brown rice flour
1/2 cup potato starch
1/4 cup tapioca flour
1/4 cup oat flour or sorghum flour (for gluten-free)
1/2 teaspoon xanthan gum
1 tablespoon Egg Replacer™
1 teaspoon baking powder
3/4 teaspoon baking soda
1/2 teaspoon cream of tartar
1/4 teaspoon salt
2/3 cup sugar
1/3 cup oil (canola or soy)
1 teaspoon vanilla extract
1/2 cup milk (rice, soy, or cow)
1/2 cup applesauce
plus
1 teaspoon cinnamon
1/4 teaspoon nutmeg
1/4 teaspoon allspice

Preheat oven to 375° F. Grease 12 muffin cups or line with baking paper.

Mix all dry ingredients thoroughly in a bowl. Make a well in the center of the dry ingredients, and then add applesauce, milk, vanilla, and oil into the well. Stir just until mixed. Pour into prepared muffin pan. Sprinkle each muffin with cinnamon sugar and bake for 15 minutes or until lightly browned.

BANANA MUFFINS

Basic Muffin Recipe (without applesauce)
1 cup brown rice flour
1/2 cup potato starch
1/4 cup tapioca flour
1/4 cup oat flour or sorghum flour (for gluten-free)
1/2 teaspoon xanthan gum
1 tablespoon Egg Replacer™
1 teaspoon baking powder
3/4 teaspoon baking soda
1/2 teaspoon cream of tartar
1/4 teaspoon salt
2/3 cup sugar
1/3 cup oil (canola or soy)
1 teaspoon vanilla extract
1/2 cup milk (rice, soy, or cow)
plus
1/2 cup bananas, mashed

Preheat oven to 375° F. Grease 12 muffin cups or line with baking paper.

Mix all dry ingredients thoroughly in a bowl. Make a well in the center of the dry ingredients, and then add bananas, milk, vanilla, and oil into the well. Stir just until mixed. Pour into prepared muffin pan. Sprinkle each muffin with sugar and bake for 15 minutes or until lightly browned.

BLUEBERRY LEMON MUFFINS

Basic Muffin Recipe
1 cup brown rice flour
1/2 cup potato starch
1/4 cup tapioca flour
1/4 cup oat flour or sorghum flour (for gluten-free)
1/2 teaspoon xanthan gum
1 tablespoon Egg Replacer™
1 teaspoon baking powder
3/4 teaspoon baking soda
1/2 teaspoon cream of tartar
1/4 teaspoon salt
2/3 cup sugar
1/3 cup oil (canola or soy)
1 teaspoon vanilla extract
1/2 cup milk (rice, soy, or cow)
1/2 cup applesauce
plus
1 cup blueberries, fresh or frozen
1 teaspoon lemon zest

Preheat oven to 375° F. Grease 12 muffin cups or line with baking paper.

To prevent the blueberry juice from coloring the batter, lightly cover blueberries in rice flour. Set aside.

Mix all dry ingredients thoroughly in a bowl. Make a well in the center of the dry ingredients, and then add applesauce, milk, vanilla, oil, and lemon zest into the well. Stir just until mixed. Gently fold in blueberries and pour into prepared muffin pan. Sprinkle each muffin with sugar and bake for 15 to 18 minutes or until lightly browned.

CARROT MUFFINS

Basic Muffin Recipe
1 cup brown rice flour
1/2 cup potato starch
1/4 cup tapioca flour
1/4 cup oat flour or sorghum flour (for gluten-free)
1/2 teaspoon xanthan gum
1 tablespoon Egg Replacer™
1 teaspoon baking powder
3/4 teaspoon baking soda
1/2 teaspoon cream of tartar
1/4 teaspoon salt
2/3 cup sugar
1/3 cup oil (canola or soy)
1 teaspoon vanilla extract
1/2 cup milk (rice, soy, or cow)
1/2 cup applesauce
plus
1 cup carrots, grated
1 teaspoon cinnamon

Preheat oven to 375° F. Grease 12 muffin cups or line with baking paper.

Mix all dry ingredients thoroughly in a bowl. Make a well in the center of the dry ingredients, and then add applesauce, milk, vanilla, oil, and carrots into the well. Stir just until mixed. Pour into prepared muffin pan. Sprinkle each muffin with cinnamon sugar and bake for 15 minutes or until lightly browned.

CRANBERRY ORANGE MUFFINS

Basic Muffin Recipe
1 cup brown rice flour
1/2 cup potato starch
1/4 cup tapioca flour
1/4 cup oat flour or sorghum flour (for gluten-free)
1/2 teaspoon xanthan gum
1 tablespoon Egg Replacer™
1 teaspoon baking powder
3/4 teaspoon baking soda
1/2 teaspoon cream of tartar
1/4 teaspoon salt
2/3 cup sugar
1/3 cup oil (canola or soy)
1 teaspoon vanilla extract
1/2 cup milk (rice, soy, or cow)
1/2 cup applesauce
plus
1 cup cranberries, fresh or frozen, chopped
1 teaspoon orange zest

Preheat oven to 375° F. Grease 12 muffin cups or line with baking paper.

To prevent the cranberry juice from coloring the batter, lightly cover cranberries in rice flour. Set aside.

Mix all dry ingredients thoroughly in a bowl. Make a well in the center of the dry ingredients, and then add applesauce, milk, vanilla, oil, and orange zest into the well. Stir just until mixed. Gently fold in cranberries and pour into prepared muffin pan. Sprinkle each muffin with sugar and bake for 15 to 18 minutes or until lightly browned.

OATMEAL CINNAMON MUFFINS

This recipe is not gluten-free.

Basic Muffin Recipe
1 cup brown rice flour
1/2 cup potato starch
1/4 cup tapioca flour
1/4 cup oat flour
1/2 teaspoon xanthan gum
1 tablespoon Egg Replacer™
1 teaspoon baking powder
3/4 teaspoon baking soda
1/2 teaspoon cream of tartar
1/4 teaspoon salt
2/3 cup sugar
1/3 cup oil (canola or soy)
1 teaspoon vanilla extract
1/2 cup milk (rice, soy, or cow)
1/2 cup applesauce
plus
1/4 cup oats
1 teaspoon cinnamon

Preheat oven to 375° F. Grease 12 muffin cups or line with baking paper.

Mix all dry ingredients thoroughly in a bowl. Make a well in the center of the dry ingredients, and then add applesauce, milk, vanilla, and oil into the well. Stir just until mixed. Pour into prepared muffin pan. Sprinkle each muffin with cinnamon sugar and bake for 15 minutes or until lightly browned.

SWEET POTATO MUFFINS

1 cup brown rice flour
1/2 cup potato starch
1/4 cup tapioca flour
1 teaspoon xanthan gum
1 tablespoon Egg Replacer™
1 teaspoon baking soda
1/8 teaspoon salt
1 teaspoon cinnamon
1/8 teaspoon nutmeg
2/3 cup brown sugar
1/3 cup oil (canola or soy)
1 teaspoon vanilla extract
1/2 cup milk (rice, soy, or cow)
1 cup sweet potatoes, baked*

Preheat oven to 375° F. Grease 12 muffin cups or line with baking paper.

Mix all dry ingredients thoroughly in a bowl. Make a well in the center of the dry ingredients, and then add sweet potatoes, milk, vanilla, and oil into the well. Stir just until mixed. Pour into prepared muffin pan. Sprinkle each muffin with cinnamon sugar and bake for 15 minutes or until lightly browned.

For baked sweet potatoes:
Preheat oven to 400° F. Wash potatoes and wrap in foil. Bake on cookie sheet until soft, about 2 hours. (Cover the pan with foil for easy clean-up, since sweet potatoes will spill sugar that burns on the pan.) Remove cooked sweet potatoes from the skins and place in a bowl.

*Tip: To minimize strings in baked sweet potatoes, remove the whole sweet potato from its skin after cooked. With a sharp paring knife, make cross-sectional cuts across the whole potato (as if cutting disks) as close together as possible. This will decrease the size of the strings so that they will not be noticed when eaten.

PUMPKIN MUFFINS

1 cup brown rice flour
1/2 cup potato starch
1/4 cup tapioca flour
1 teaspoon xanthan gum
1 tablespoon Egg Replacer™
1 teaspoon baking soda
1/8 teaspoon salt
1 teaspoon cinnamon
1/8 teaspoon ginger
1/8 teaspoon nutmeg
2/3 cup brown sugar
1/3 cup oil (canola or soy)
1 teaspoon vanilla extract
1/2 cup milk (rice, soy, or cow)
1 cup pumpkin puree

Preheat oven to 375° F. Grease 12 muffin cups or line with baking paper.

Mix all dry ingredients thoroughly in a bowl. Make a well in the center of the dry ingredients, and then add pumpkin, milk, vanilla, and oil into the well. Stir just until mixed. Pour into prepared muffin pan. Sprinkle each muffin with cinnamon sugar and bake for 15 minutes or until lightly browned.

DOUBLE CHOCOLATE CHIP MUFFINS

1 cup brown rice flour
1/2 cup potato starch
1/4 cup tapioca flour
1/4 cup cocoa
1/2 teaspoon xanthan gum
1 tablespoon Egg Replacer™
1 teaspoon baking powder
1/2 teaspoon baking soda
1/4 teaspoon salt
1 cup sugar
1/2 cup oil (canola or soy)
1 teaspoon vanilla extract
3/4 cup milk (rice, soy, or cow)
1/4 cup applesauce
1/2 cup semi-sweet chocolate chips

Preheat oven to 375° F. Grease 12 muffin cups or line with baking
paper.

Mix all dry ingredients thoroughly in a bowl. Make a well in the center
of the dry ingredients, and then add applesauce, milk, vanilla, and oil
into the well. Stir just until mixed. Gently fold in chocolate chips.
Pour into prepared muffin pan and bake for 18 minutes.

CORN MEAL MUFFINS

1/2 cup brown rice flour
1/2 cup potato starch
1/2 cup tapioca flour
1/2 cup corn meal
1/2 teaspoon xanthan gum
2 teaspoons Egg Replacer™
2 teaspoons baking powder
1/2 teaspoon baking soda
1/2 cup sugar
1/2 cup oil (canola or soy)
3/4 cup milk (rice, soy, or cow)
2 tablespoons applesauce
1 tablespoon lemon juice

Preheat oven to 375° F. Grease 12 muffin cups or line with baking paper.

Mix all dry ingredients thoroughly in a bowl. Make a well in the center of the dry ingredients, and then add applesauce, milk, oil, and lemon juice into the well. Stir just until mixed. Pour into prepared muffin pan and bake for 15 minutes or until lightly browned.

CRANBERRY ORANGE BREAD

2/3 cup brown rice flour
2/3 cup potato starch
2/3 cup tapioca flour
1 teaspoon xanthan gum
1 1/2 teaspoons Egg Replacer™
1 1/2 teaspoons baking powder
1/2 teaspoon baking soda
1 teaspoon salt
3/4 cup sugar
2 tablespoons oil (canola or soy)
2 tablespoons applesauce
3/4 cup orange juice (preferably fresh squeezed)
1 cup cranberries, chopped
1 teaspoon orange zest

Preheat oven to 350° F. Grease loaf pan or mini-loaf pan.

Mix all dry ingredients thoroughly in a bowl. Mix orange juice, orange zest, applesauce, and oil in another bowl. Add wet ingredients to dry ingredients and stir just until mixed. Gently fold in cranberries and pour into prepared pan. Bake 20 minutes for mini loaves or 55 minutes for average-sized loaf, until lightly brown and toothpick inserted in center comes out clean. Cool on rack.

Optional glaze: Mix 1/4 cup confectioners' sugar, 1/2 teaspoon corn syrup, and enough milk or water to make glaze consistency. Drizzle glaze on top of cool loaf.

ZUCCHINI BREAD

1/2 cup brown rice flour
1/2 cup potato starch
1/4 cup tapioca flour
1/4 cup oat flour or sorghum flour (for gluten-free)
1 teaspoon xanthan gum
1 1/2 tablespoons Egg Replacer™
1/4 teaspoon baking powder
1/2 teaspoon baking soda
1/2 teaspoon salt
1 teaspoon cinnamon
1/2 teaspoon nutmeg
1 cup sugar
1/4 cup oil (canola or soy)
2 tablespoons applesauce
2 tablespoons water
1 cup zucchini, finely shredded
1/4 teaspoon lemon zest

Preheat oven to 350° F. Grease loaf pan or mini-loaf pan.

Mix all dry ingredients, except sugar, thoroughly in a bowl. Mix all remaining ingredients thoroughly in another bowl. Add wet ingredients to dry ingredients and stir just until mixed. Pour into prepared pan. Bake 20 minutes for mini loaves or 55 minutes for average-sized loaf, until lightly brown and toothpick inserted in center comes out clean. Cool on rack.

COMMENTS

CHAPTER 4
BREADS

Yeast Dough
Rolls
Breadsticks and Pretzels
Yeast-free Breadsticks
Cornbread
Corn Cakes
Hush Puppies
Savory Corn Fritters
Plain Biscuits
Cinnamon Biscuits
Sweet Potato Biscuits
Tortillas

The savory flavor of these breads makes each a great addition to meals.

YEAST DOUGH

1 package yeast
1/3 cup brown rice flour
1/3 cup potato starch
1/3 cup tapioca flour
1 tablespoon sweet white rice flour
1/4 teaspoon Dough Enhancer™*
2 teaspoons xanthan gum
1 1/4 teaspoons gelatin or Agar
1/2 teaspoon salt
1/2 teaspoon sugar
1 tablespoon olive oil
1 teaspoon vinegar
1/2 cup very warm water

Preheat oven to 400° F.

Mix all dry ingredients together in a bowl. Use an electric mixer to beat together oil, vinegar, and warm water. Add just enough water to make the dough sticky and smooth. The dough should wrap around the beaters. If the dough is too stiff, add water a tablespoon at a time. Beat for about 2 minutes.

*Note: Dough Enhancer contains soy lecithin. If you are avoiding soy lecithin, then omit from the recipe. The texture of the dough will not be quite as smooth as with it; however, the taste will be just as good.

YEAST ROLLS

Turn dough out onto floured surface. Use tapioca or potato starch. Knead 2 or 3 times to make smooth dough. Use hands to press dough out to 1/4" thick. Cut rolls with well floured biscuit cutter and place on lightly greased baking sheet. Brush tops of rolls with olive oil and allow rolls to rise for 15 minutes. Bake 15 to 20 minutes or until golden brown.

BREADSTICKS and PRETZELS

Preheat oven to 400° F.
Prepare Yeast Dough Recipe on page 50.

Tip: Plastic decorator bags and decorator tips make this recipe a lot easier, since you can vary the sizes without changing bags. Instructions include tip sizes if you have these tools. Otherwise, freezer bags work just fine. Just start with the smallest size you want first. Then cut the opening bigger as desired.

Lightly coat the inside of a freezer bag or decorator bag with olive oil or cooking spray. Add dough to the bag. Squeeze the dough out as directed below onto a lightly greased baking sheet. Spray the tops with cooking spray. Sprinkle with kosher salt and bake until golden brown and crunchy. Rotate during baking to ensure even browning.

For breadsticks: Cut 1/4" opening to make 1/2" diameter breadsticks or use a coupler without a decorator tip. Bake 15 to 25 minutes.

For pretzel rods: Cut 1/8" opening to make 1/4" diameter pretzel rods or use a #12 decorator tip. Bake 10 to 20 minutes

For pretzel sticks: Cut 1/16" opening to make 1/8" diameter pretzel sticks or use a #6 decorator tip. Bake 8 to 12 minutes.

*Note: The dough is too sticky to be brushed with oil. If commercial cooking sprays are not appropriate for your diet, try using a non-aerosol pump filled with olive oil to spray the oil onto the dough.

YEAST-FREE BREADSTICKS

1/4 cup brown rice flour
1/4 cup potato starch
1/4 cup tapioca flour
1 tablespoon sweet white rice flour
1 tablespoon barley flour or brown rice flour (for gluten-free)
1/4 teaspoon Dough Enhancer™*
1/2 teaspoon xanthan gum
3/4 teaspoon baking powder
1/4 teaspoon salt
1 1/2 tablespoons shortening
1 tablespoon olive oil
1/4 cup cold water

Preheat oven to 350° F.

Mix dry ingredients well in a bowl. Use a fork or pastry cutter to cut in shortening and olive oil. Stir in water slowly until a ball forms.

Turn dough out onto a surface lightly floured with tapioca flour. Use fingers to gently press dough into a rectangle 1/4" thick. Cut dough into strips with a pastry scraper or pizza roller. Gently roll each strip to form a breadstick.

Place breadsticks on a baking sheet. Spray the tops with cooking spray or brush with olive oil. Sprinkle with kosher salt and bake 15 minutes or until crisp.

*Note: Dough Enhancer contains soy lecithin. If you are avoiding soy lecithin, then omit from the recipe. The texture of the dough will not be quite as smooth as with it; however, the taste will be just as good.

CORNBREAD

1/4 cup brown rice flour
1/2 cup potato starch
1/4 cup tapioca flour
1/4 cup corn flour
3/4 cup corn meal
1 teaspoon xanthan gum
1 1/2 teaspoons Egg Replacer™
2 teaspoons baking powder
1/2 teaspoon salt
1/4 cup sugar
1/4 cup oil (canola or soy)
1 cup milk (rice, soy, or cow)
1/4 cup applesauce

Preheat oven to 375° F. Grease 1 8" cake pan or 2 6" cake pans.

Mix all dry ingredients thoroughly in a bowl. Make a well in the center of the dry ingredients, and then add applesauce, milk, and oil into the well. Stir just until mixed. Pour into prepared pan(s) and bake for 20 minutes or until lightly browned.

CORN CAKES

1 cup masa
1/4 cup tapioca flour
1/4 cup sweet white rice flour
1/4 teaspoon xanthan gum
1 teaspoon baking powder
1/2 teaspoon salt
2 tablespoons shortening
1 cup warm water
oil for frying

Fill oil about 1/2" deep in skillet. Preheat oil on medium heat.

Combine dry ingredients in a bowl. Use a fork or pastry cutter to cut shortening into the dry mixture with a fork. Add water to form a smooth ball. Form 2" balls with wet hands. Flatten out to form 1/4" thick cakes and fry in oil in preheated skillet until golden brown on both sides. Drain on paper towels.

HUSH PUPPIES

1/4 cup brown rice flour
1/4 cup potato starch
1/4 cup tapioca flour
1/8 cup corn flour
1/8 cup sweet white rice flour
1/2 teaspoon xanthan gum
1 1/2 teaspoons Egg Replacer™
1 1/2 teaspoons baking powder
1/4 teaspoon salt
1/8 teaspoon onion powder (optional)
3 tablespoons sugar
1/2 to 3/4 cup milk (rice, soy, or cow)
oil for frying

Fill oil about 2" deep in pot. Preheat oil to 360° F using frying thermometer. Leave the thermometer in during cooking as well.

Combine dry ingredients in a bowl. Add just enough milk to make a smooth but thick batter. Carefully drop teaspoonfuls into hot oil. Cook until deep golden brown on both sides, about 1 minute. Remove from oil and drain on paper towel.

Note: Be sure to keep oil temperature around 360°F. If the oil gets too hot, the outside of the hush puppies will cook too fast, leaving raw dough on the inside. If the oil gets too cool, the hush puppies will absorb the oil and will taste greasy.

SAVORY CORN FRITTERS

Follow recipe for Hush Puppies except:
        omit onion powder
        add 1/2 cup frozen corn, thawed, to batter.
Follow the same cooking directions.

PLAIN BISCUITS

1/3 cup brown rice flour
1/3 cup potato starch
1/3 cup tapioca flour
1/4 teaspoon xanthan gum
1 1/2 teaspoons baking powder
1/4 teaspoon cream of tartar
1/8 teaspoon salt
1 teaspoon sugar
1/4 cup shortening
1/3 milk (rice, soy, or cow)

Preheat oven to 450° F.

Combine dry ingredients in a bowl. Use a fork or pastry cutter to cut shortening into the flour mixture. Add milk and stir. Lightly dust surface with tapioca flour or potato starch. Gently press out dough with hands to 1/2" thick. Cut with biscuit cutter and place on ungreased cookie sheet. Bake 10 to 12 minutes or until lightly brown.

CINNAMON BISCUITS

Follow recipe for Plain Biscuits and add:
    1/2 teaspoon cinnamon and
    1/8 teaspoon nutmeg to dry mixture
Follow the same cooking directions.

SWEET POTATO BISCUITS

1 cup brown rice flour
1/2 cup potato starch
1/4 cup tapioca flour
1 teaspoon xanthan gum
1 tablespoon baking powder
1/2 teaspoon salt
1/2 teaspoon cinnamon
1/8 teaspoon nutmeg
1/2 cup brown sugar
1/2 cup margarine
2 tablespoons milk (rice, soy, or cow)
1/2 teaspoon vanilla
1 cup sweet potatoes, baked*

Preheat oven to 375° F.

Combine all dry ingredients in a bowl. Use a fork or pastry cutter to cut margarine or shortening into flour mixture. Stir in milk, vanilla, and sweet potatoes. Lightly dust surface with tapioca flour or potato starch. Gently roll out dough to 1/2" thick. Cut with biscuit cutter and place on ungreased cookie sheet. Brush tops with melted margarine or olive oil to brown. Bake 10 to 12 minutes or until lightly brown on bottom.

For baked sweet potatoes:
Preheat oven to 400° F. Wash potatoes and wrap in foil. Bake on cookie sheet until soft, about 2 hours. (Cover the pan with foil for easy clean-up, since sweet potatoes will spill sugar that burns on the pan.) Remove cooked sweet potatoes from the skins and place in a bowl.

*Tip: To minimize strings in baked sweet potatoes, remove whole sweet potato from skin after cooked. With sharp paring knife, make cross-sectional cuts across the whole potato (as if cutting disks) as close together as possible. This will decrease the size of the strings so that they will not be noticed when eaten.

TORTILLAS

1/4 cup brown rice flour
1/4 cup potato starch
1/4 cup tapioca flour
1 teaspoon baking powder
1/4 teaspoon salt
1/4 cup margarine or shortening
1/4 to 1/2 cup water

Preheat skillet to medium.

Combine all dry ingredients. Use a fork or pastry cutter to cut margarine or shortening into flour mixture. Add just enough water to make stiff dough. Turn dough out onto well-floured surface. Roll out as thin as possible. Cook on preheated skillet until lightly brown on both sides.

Makes 6 to 8.

COMMENTS

CHAPTER 5
CRACKERS

Rice Crackers
Barley Crackers
"Graham" Crackers

Crackers are great snack foods that will keep fresh for several days in an airtight bag or container.

RICE CRACKERS

1 1/2 cups brown rice flour
1/2 cup potato starch
1/8 cup tapioca flour
1/4 cup oat flour or sorghum flour (for gluten-free)
3/4 teaspoon xanthan gum
1 teaspoon baking powder
1/2 teaspoon baking soda
1/2 teaspoon salt
1 tablespoon sugar
1/2 cup margarine or shortening
4 tablespoons water, ice cold

Preheat oven to 325° F. Cover a cookie sheet with parchment paper.

Combine all dry ingredients in a bowl. Use a fork or pastry cutter to cut margarine or shortening into the flour mixture. Add enough water to form a smooth ball. Lightly dust surface with tapioca flour. Divide dough in half.

Roll out dough to 1/8" thick. Cut into 2" squares and place on prepared cookie sheet. Use a fork to prick holes in each cracker. Sprinkle salt (preferably kosher or sea salt) on tops, if desired. Bake 12 to 15 minutes or until lightly brown on bottom. Repeat for second half of dough.

BARLEY CRACKERS

This recipe is not gluten-free.

1/2 cup brown rice flour
1/2 cup potato starch
1/4 cup tapioca flour
1 cup barley flour
1/2 teaspoon barley malt extract (optional)
3/4 teaspoon xanthan gum
1 teaspoon baking powder
1/2 teaspoon baking soda
1/2 teaspoon salt
1 tablespoon sugar
1/2 cup margarine or shortening
3 to 4 tablespoons water, ice cold

Preheat oven to 325° F. Cover a cookie sheet with parchment paper.

Combine all dry ingredients in a bowl. Use a fork or pastry cutter to cut margarine or shortening into the flour mixture. Add enough water to form a smooth ball. Lightly dust surface with tapioca flour. Divide dough in half.

Roll out dough to 1/8" thick. Cut into 2" squares and place on prepared cookie sheet. Use a fork to prick holes in each cracker. Sprinkle salt (preferably kosher or sea salt) on tops, if desired. Bake 12 to 15 minutes or until lightly brown on bottom. Repeat for second half of dough.

"GRAHAM" CRACKERS

1 1/2 cups brown rice flour
1/2 cup potato starch
1/8 cup tapioca flour
1/4 cup oat flour or sorghum flour (for gluten-free)
3/4 teaspoon xanthan gum
1 teaspoon baking powder
1/2 teaspoon baking soda
1/2 teaspoon salt
2 teaspoons cinnamon
1/2 cup brown sugar
1/2 cup margarine
1 teaspoon vanilla
2 tablespoons light corn syrup
4 tablespoons water, ice cold

Preheat oven to 325° F. Cover two cookie sheets with parchment paper.

Combine all dry ingredients in a bowl. Use a fork or pastry cutter to cut margarine into the flour mixture. Add vanilla, corn syrup, and enough water for dough to begin to stick together. Press the dough in hands to form two balls.

Roll out dough to 1/8" thick between two sheets of wax paper, lightly dusted with tapioca flour. Cut into 2" squares and place on prepared cookie sheet. Use a fork to prick holes in each cracker. Sprinkle tops with cinnamon sugar. Bake 12 to 15 minutes or until lightly brown on bottom. Repeat for second half of dough.

COMMENTS

CHAPTER 6
MEAT and POTATOES

Pot Pie Biscuit Topping
Pot Pie Crust Topping
Chicken/Turkey Pot Pie
Corn Dog Batter
Potato Cakes
Hashed Brown Potatoes
Mashed Potatoes
Mashed Sweet Potatoes
Creamed Corn

There are countless recipes with meats and vegetables that do not contain the foods this cookbook is avoiding. This cookbook does not recreate these kinds of recipes. Instead, the recipes in this chapter are intended to be those popular foods that people usually love, but cannot buy commercially because of food allergies. Each recipe is easy to prepare and is great as either a main dish or as a side item.

POT PIE BISCUIT TOPPING

1/4 cup brown rice flour
1/4 cup potato starch
1/4 cup tapioca flour
1/4 cup sweet white rice flour
1/4 teaspoon xanthan gum
1 1/2 teaspoons Egg Replacer™
1 1/2 teaspoons baking powder
1/2 teaspoon salt
1/4 cup margarine
1/4 cup milk (rice, soy, or cow)

Combine dry ingredients in a bowl. Use a fork or pastry cutter to cut margarine into the dry ingredients. Stir in milk to form a loose ball. Spread topping over the pot pie filling (see page 70).

Bake at 450° F for 10 to 12 minutes.

POT PIE CRUST TOPPING

1/2 cup brown rice flour
1/2 cup potato starch
1/4 cup tapioca flour
1/4 cup sweet white rice flour
1/2 teaspoon xanthan gum
1 tablespoon Egg Replacer™
2 teaspoons baking powder
1/2 teaspoon salt
1/4 cup margarine
1/2 cup milk (rice, soy, or cow)

Combine dry ingredients in a bowl. Use a fork or pastry cutter to cut margarine into the dry ingredients. Stir in milk to form a smooth ball. Roll out dough to 1/8" thick on wax paper dusted with tapioca starch. Carefully place dough over the pot pie filling (see page 70). Cut slits in dough to vent steam.

Bake at 450° F for 10 to 12 minutes.

CHICKEN/TURKEY POT PIE

1 cup peas, frozen
1 cup diced carrots, frozen
1 cup corn, frozen
2 tablespoons margarine
1/4 cup potato starch
1 teaspoon salt
1/4 teaspoon pepper
1 1/3 cups low sodium chicken broth
1/4 cup milk (rice, soy, cow)
2 cups cooked chicken breast or turkey breast, cubed
Pot Pie Biscuit topping (see page 68) *or*
Pot Pie Crust topping (see page 69)

Preheat oven to 450° F.

Cook frozen vegetables together as directed by package. Drain and set aside.

Combine milk and chicken broth. Set aside. Melt margarine in skillet. Stir in potato starch and seasonings. Add milk mixture to skillet a little at a time, stirring well after each addition. Make sure starch and milk are smooth before adding more of the milk mixture. After all the liquid is incorporated, cook gently until thickened and bubbly, about 1 to 2 minutes. Stir in vegetables and chicken. Pour into an 8"x8" casserole dish and cover with pot pie topping of choice. Place the casserole dish on a baking pan to catch any spills and bake 10 to 12 minutes.

CORN DOGS

1/4 cup brown rice flour
1/4 cup potato starch
1/4 cup tapioca flour
1/8 cup corn flour
1/8 cup sweet white rice flour
1/2 teaspoon xanthan gum
1 1/2 teaspoons Egg Replacer™
1 1/2 teaspoons baking powder
1/4 teaspoon salt
3 tablespoons sugar
1/2 to 3/4 cup milk (rice, soy, or cow)
hotdogs on a stick, little wieners or vegetarian substitute
oil for frying

Fill oil about 2" deep in a 2-quart pot. Preheat oil to 360° F using frying thermometer. Leave the thermometer in place during cooking.

Combine dry ingredients in a bowl. Add just enough milk to make smooth but thick batter. Dip hotdogs, wieners, or vegetarian substitute into batter, completely coating entire surface. Carefully drop into hot oil. Cook until deep golden brown, about 1 minute. Remove from oil and drain on paper towel.

Note: Be sure to keep oil temperature around 360°F. If the oil gets too hot, the outside of the corndog will cook too fast, leaving raw dough on the inside. If the oil gets too cool, the corndog will absorb the oil and will taste greasy.

Caution: Be sure that any meat product is free of unwanted ingredients. Many processed meats contain dairy, wheat, gluten, or soy products.

POTATO CAKES

2 potatoes, peeled, grated, rinsed, and dried
1 tablespoon brown rice flour
1 tablespoon tapioca starch or potato starch
1/4 teaspoon Egg Replacer™
1/2 teaspoon baking powder
1/2 teaspoon salt
1 tablespoon warm water

Fill oil about 1/8" deep in a skillet. Preheat on medium.

Combine ingredients in a bowl. Drop tablespoonful-sized cakes in oil and flatten. Fry until golden brown on both sides. Drain on paper towels. Sprinkle with salt as desired.

HASHED BROWN POTATOES

2 to 3 baking potatoes, peeled, diced, rinsed
salt
canola or soy oil

Bring a large stock pot of lightly salted water to a boil. Add potatoes and return to a slow boil. Cook until pieces are almost fork tender. To stop the potatoes from cooking, drain and immediately pour into a large bowl of iced water for about 2 minutes, or until cool but not cold. Drain again and pat dry with paper towels.

Fill oil about 1" deep in a skillet. Preheat oil to 375° F. Place small batches of potatoes in oil. (Use caution since water in potatoes may cause the oil to splatter.) Cook until golden brown. Drain on paper towels and sprinkle with salt as desired. Allow oil to return to 375° F before cooking remaining batches.

MASHED POTATOES

4 to 5 baking potatoes, peeled, diced, rinsed
margarine
milk (rice, soy, or cow) or cream

To prevent potatoes from browning, keep peeled potatoes in cold water until ready to cook. Cut potatoes into uniform cubes to ensure all pieces cook at the same rate.

Fill a large stock pot with just enough water to cover the potatoes. Add salt to the water to suit taste preference. It is important to salt the water before cooking the potatoes since the potatoes will not absorb the flavor after cooking.

Bring water and potatoes to a gentle boil. Boiling too fast may water-log potatoes, causing them to fall apart and taste mushy. Boil until potato cubes are fork tender. Drain water and return potatoes to the cooking pot. Stir together potatoes, about 1 tablespoon of margarine, and enough milk or cream to make creamy.

For Garlic Mashed Potatoes:

Prepare Mashed Potatoes as above *and...*
About 1 hour before making mashed potatoes, coat a whole garlic head in olive oil and cover in foil. Roast the garlic head in a 400°F oven for about 1 hour, or until very soft. Carefully cut top of garlic head off and squeeze contents into mashed potatoes. Blend well.

MASHED SWEET POTATOES

2 large sweet potatoes
3/8 cup brown sugar
1/2 teaspoon cinnamon
1 to 2 tablespoons milk (rice, soy, or cow)

Preheat oven to 400° F. Wash potatoes and wrap each in foil. Bake on a cookie sheet until soft, about 2 hours. (Cover the pan with foil for easy clean-up, since sweet potatoes will spill sugar that burns on the pan.)

Remove cooked sweet potatoes from the skins and place in a bowl. Add brown sugar, cinnamon, and milk. Beat with mixer until creamy.

*Tip: To minimize strings in mashed sweet potatoes, remove whole sweet potato from skin after cooked. With sharp paring knife, make cross-sectional cuts across the whole potato (as if cutting disks) as close together as possible. This will decrease the size of the strings so that they will not be noticed when eaten.

CREAMED CORN

2 tablespoons margarine
2 tablespoons tapioca flour
1 cup milk (rice, soy, or cow)
2 cups frozen corn, thawed, or fresh removed from ears
salt to taste
1/4 cup frozen diced carrots, thawed (optional)
1/4 cup frozen peas, thawed (optional)

Preheat skillet on medium heat. Melt margarine. Whisk in tapioca flour until combined. Add milk to skillet a little at a time, stirring well after each addition. Make sure flour and milk are smooth before adding more milk. After all milk is incorporated, cook gently until thickened and bubbly. Add corn and simmer 3 to 4 minutes. Add salt to taste.

COMMENTS

CHAPTER 7
COOKIES and BARS

Gluten-free Cookie Flour Mix
Sugar Cookies
Iced Cutout Cookies
Chocolate Chip Cookies
Double Chocolate Chip Cookies
Oatmeal Cookies
Apple-filled Oatmeal Cookies
Glazed Apple Spice Cookies
Snickerdoodle Cookies
Vanilla Cream Cookies
Chocolate Cream Cookies
Lemon Cream Cookies
Jelly Roll Cookies
Cinnamon Roll Cookies
Press Cookies
Fudge Brownies
Granola Bars

I just love these cookie recipes because they taste just like the cookies I have always enjoyed. Some people have even told me that they could not tell these treats were made without wheat!

GLUTEN-FREE COOKIE FLOUR MIX

2 cups brown rice flour
2 cups potato starch
1 cup tapioca starch
1 cup sweet white rice flour

Thoroughly combine all ingredients and store in an airtight container or zippered plastic bag in a cool, dry place.

Makes 6 cups

SUGAR COOKIES

1 1/2 cups Gluten-free Cookie Flour Mix (see page 80)
1/4 cup tapioca flour
3/4 teaspoon xanthan gum
1 1/2 tablespoons Egg Replacer™
1 teaspoon baking powder
1/4 teaspoon salt
1 cup sugar
1/2 cup margarine
1/2 teaspoon vanilla
3 to 4 tablespoons water

Preheat oven to 375°F. Cover a cookie sheet with parchment paper.

Combine dry ingredients, except sugar, in a bowl and set aside. In another bowl, beat margarine and sugar with an electric mixer until creamy. Add vanilla and 3 tablespoons of water. Add dry ingredients. If dough is too dry, add an additional tablespoon of water just until dough comes together.

Turn out dough onto wax paper to form a 12" log. Wrap with wax paper and chill 30 minutes in the freezer. Cut into 1/2" disks and place on the prepared cookie sheet. If desired, sprinkle with colored sugar crystals. Bake 10 to 12 minutes or until just beginning to brown. Cool on pan for 1 minute and transfer to cooling rack.

Makes 2 to 3 dozen.

ICED CUTOUT COOKIES

1 1/2 cups Gluten-free Cookie Flour Mix (see page 80)
3/4 teaspoon xanthan gum
1 teaspoon Egg Replacer™
1 teaspoon baking powder
1/2 cup sugar
1/2 cup margarine
1/2 teaspoon vanilla
2 to 3 tablespoons water
*can be tinted with food coloring if desired

Icing:
1 cup confectioners' sugar
2 teaspoons milk (rice, soy, or cow)
2 teaspoons light corn syrup
* can be tinted with food coloring if desired

Preheat oven to 375°F. Cover a cookie sheet with parchment paper.

For cookies: Combine dry ingredients, except sugar, in a bowl and set aside. In another bowl, beat margarine and sugar with an electric mixer until creamy. Add vanilla, 2 tablespoons of water, and food coloring (if desired). Add dry ingredients. If dough is too dry, add an additional tablespoon of water just until dough comes together.

Roll out dough to 1/8" thick between two sheets of wax paper, lightly dusted with potato or tapioca starch. Use cookie cutters or a biscuit cutter to form cookies. Carefully transfer to the prepared cookie sheet. (Tip: Lightly dust a pastry scraper to help pick up the cookies.) Bake 6 to 7 minutes or until just beginning to brown. Cool on pan for 1 minute and transfer to cooling rack. After cooled, cover cookies with icing.

For icing: Mix confectioners' sugar and milk. Then add corn syrup and food coloring (if desired).

Makes 2 dozen.

CHOCOLATE CHIP COOKIES

2 1/4 cups Gluten-free Cookie Flour Mix (see page 80)
1/4 cup tapioca flour
1/2 teaspoon xanthan gum
2 teaspoons Egg Replacer™
1/2 teaspoon baking powder
1/2 teaspoon baking soda
1/2 teaspoon salt
2/3 cup sugar
1/3 cup brown sugar
1/2 cup margarine
3/4 teaspoon vanilla
2 to 4 tablespoons water
1 cup semi-sweet chocolate chips

Preheat oven to 375°F. Cover a cookie sheet with parchment paper.

Combine dry ingredients, except sugars, in a bowl and set aside. In another bowl, beat margarine and sugars with an electric mixer until creamy. Add vanilla and 2 tablespoons of water. Add dry ingredients. If dough is too dry, add just enough water for dough to form a stiff ball. Then stir in chocolate chips by hand.

Form 1" balls, flatten slightly, and place on the prepared cookie sheet. (Tip: Scoop out dough using a 1" melon baller and then roll dough into a ball using hands.) Bake 9 minutes. Cool on pan for 2 minutes and transfer to cooling rack.

Makes 4 dozen.

DOUBLE CHOCOLATE CHIP COOKIES

1 1/2 cups Gluten-free Cookie Flour Mix (see page 80)
1/4 cup cocoa, sifted
1/4 teaspoon xanthan gum
1 teaspoon Egg Replacer™
1/4 teaspoon baking soda
1/4 teaspoon salt
1/2 cup sugar
1/4 cup brown sugar
1/4 cup margarine
1/4 cup shortening
1 teaspoon vanilla
1/2 cup milk (rice, soy, or cow)
1/2 cup semi-sweet chocolate chips

Preheat oven to 375°F. Cover a cookie sheet with parchment paper.

Combine dry ingredients, except sugars, in a bowl and set aside. In another bowl, beat margarine and shortening with an electric mixer until blended. Then add sugars and beat until creamy. Add vanilla and milk. Add dry ingredients. Stir in chocolate chips by hand.

Divide dough in half. Turn out each half onto wax paper to form two 8" log. Chill 30 minutes in the freezer. Cut into 1/4" disks and place on the prepared cookie sheet. Bake 10 to 12 minutes. Cool on pan for 1 minute and transfer to cooling rack.

Makes 2 dozen.

OATMEAL COOKIES

This recipe is not gluten-free.

1/2 cup brown rice flour
1/2 cup oat flour
1/2 teaspoon xanthan gum
3/4 teaspoon baking soda
1/8 teaspoon cream of tartar
1/4 teaspoon salt
1/2 teaspoon cinnamon
1/2 cup sugar
1/4 cup brown sugar
1/2 cup margarine
1 teaspoon vanilla
3 tablespoons milk (rice, soy, or cow)
1 cup oats

Preheat oven to 375°F. Cover a cookie sheet with parchment paper.

Combine dry ingredients, except oats and sugars, in a bowl and set aside. In another bowl, beat margarine and sugars with an electric mixer until creamy. Add milk and vanilla. Add dry ingredients and mix. Then add oats.

Use 1" melon baller to measure each cookie. Drop onto the prepared cookie sheet about 2" apart. Bake 8 to 9 minutes. Cool on pan for 1 minute and transfer to cooling rack.

Makes 2 dozen.

APPLE-FILLED OATMEAL COOKIES

This recipe is not gluten-free.

1/4 cup brown rice flour
1/4 cup oat flour
1/4 cup tapioca flour
1/4 cup sweet white rice flour
1/4 teaspoon xanthan gum
1 1/2 teaspoons Egg Replacer™
1 teaspoon baking powder
1/2 teaspoon cinnamon
1/8 teaspoon nutmeg
1/8 teaspoon salt
1/2 cup brown sugar
1/2 cup margarine
1/4 teaspoon vanilla
1/4 cup milk (rice, soy, or cow)
3/4 cup oats
Apple filling (see page 87)

Preheat oven to 375°F. Cover a cookie sheet with parchment paper.

Prepare apple filling as directed. Let cool.

Combine dry ingredients, except oats and sugars, in a bowl and set aside. In another bowl, beat margarine and sugar with an electric mixer until creamy. Add milk and vanilla. Add dry ingredients and mix. Then add oats.

Drop tablespoon-sized cookies 1 1/2" apart onto the prepared cookie sheet. Add filling to center of each cookie. Bake 10 to 12 minutes. Cool on pan for 1 minute and transfer to cooling rack.

Makes 2 dozen.

APPLE FILLING for
APPLE-FILLED OATMEAL COOKIES

1 1/2 cups cooking apples, peeled, cored, and diced
1/3 cup sugar
1/3 cup raisins (optional)
2 tablespoons water
1 to 2 teaspoons tapioca starch

Combine apples, sugar, raisins, and water in small sauce pot on medium heat. Bring to a gentle boil and cook until apples are tender.

After apples are tender, add small amount of hot liquid from apples to the starch and mix. Then add the starch mixture back to the sauce and stir until thickened. Remove from heat and cool. Add to cookies as directed on page 86.

GLAZED APPLE SPICE COOKIES

2 cups Gluten-free Cookie Flour Mix (see page 80)
1/2 teaspoon xanthan gum
1 1/2 teaspoons Egg Replacer™
1 teaspoon baking soda
1 teaspoon cinnamon
1/4 teaspoon nutmeg
1/4 teaspoon cloves
1/2 teaspoon salt
1 cup brown sugar
1/4 cup margarine
1/4 cup shortening
1/2 teaspoon vanilla
1/4 cup milk (rice, soy, or cow)
1 cup cooking apples, peeled, cored, and finely diced

Glaze:
1 1/2 cups confectioners' sugar
1 tablespoon margarine
1/2 teaspoon vanilla
2 tablespoons milk (rice, soy, or cow)

Preheat oven to 375°F. Cover cookie sheet with parchment paper.

Combine dry ingredients, except sugar, in a bowl and set aside. In
another bowl, beat margarine and shortening with an electric mixer
until blended. Then add sugar and beat until creamy. Add milk and
vanilla. Add dry ingredients and mix. Stir in apples by hand.

Drop tablespoon-sized cookies 1 1/2" apart onto the prepared cookie
sheet. Bake 10-12 minutes. Cool on pan for 1 minute and transfer to
cooling rack.

For glaze: Use an electric mixer to all ingredients until smooth. Add
just enough milk to make it a good spreading consistency. Spread onto
warm cookies.

Makes 2 dozen.

SNICKERDOODLE COOKIES

2 1/4 cups Gluten-free Cookie Flour Mix (see page 80)
3/4 teaspoon xanthan gum
1 1/2 teaspoons Egg Replacer™
1/4 teaspoon baking powder
1/4 teaspoon baking soda
1/4 teaspoon cream of tartar
1/2 teaspoon salt
1 cup sugar
1/2 cup margarine
1/2 teaspoon vanilla
2 to 3 tablespoons milk (rice, soy, or cow)

Cinnamon Sugar:
1 1/2 tablespoons sugar
1/2 teaspoon cinnamon

Preheat oven to 375°F. Cover a cookie sheet with parchment paper.

Combine dry ingredients, except sugar, in a bowl and set aside. In another bowl, beat margarine and sugar with an electric mixer until creamy. Add vanilla and 2 tablespoons of milk. Add dry ingredients. If dough is too dry, add just enough milk for dough to form a stiff ball.

Form 1" balls. (Tip: Scoop out dough using a 1" melon baller and then roll dough into a ball using hands.) Chill balls for 30 minutes in the freezer. Roll each ball in cinnamon sugar mixture and place on the prepared cookie sheet. Bake 8 minutes or until just beginning to brown. Cool on pan for 1 minute and transfer to cooling rack.

Makes 3 dozen.

VANILLA CREAM COOKIES

2 1/4 cups Gluten-free Cookie Flour Mix (see page 80)
1 teaspoon xanthan gum
1/2 teaspoon baking powder
1/4 teaspoon baking soda
1/4 teaspoon cream of tartar
1/4 teaspoon salt
3/4 cup sugar
1/2 cup shortening
1 teaspoon vanilla
1 tablespoon corn syrup
2 to 4 tablespoons water
Cream filling (see page 91)

Preheat oven to 325°F. Cover a cookie sheet with parchment paper.

Prepare cream filling as directed.

Combine dry ingredients in a bowl and mix thoroughly. Use a fork or pastry cutter to cut shortening into flour mixture. In a small bowl, combine vanilla, corn syrup, and 2 tablespoons of water. Add to dry mixture to form smooth ball. If dough is too dry, add just enough water for dough to form a smooth ball. Divide dough in half and wrap each half in plastic wrap. Chill in the freezer for 30 minutes.

Lightly dust wax paper with tapioca flour. Roll out to 1/8"-1/4" thickness. Use biscuit cutter to cut out cookies. Transfer to the prepared cookie sheet. (Tip: Use a pastry scraper or thin metal spatula to help lift up cookies.) Use a fork to prick holes in each cookie. Sprinkle with sugar and bake for 10 minutes or until just turning brown on edges. Cool on pan 1 minute and transfer to cooling rack.

After cookies are cool, spread filling on underside of one cookie and cover with underside of another to form a "sandwich." Repeat for remaining cookies.

Makes 2 dozen.

CREAM FILLING
for VANILLA CREAM COOKIES

1/2 cup shortening
2 cups confectioners' sugar
1 teaspoon vanilla
3 to 4 tablespoons water

Use an electric mixer to beat shortening, vanilla, and 2 tablespoons of water. Gradually add sugar. If too thick, add just enough water to form a very stiff filling.

CHOCOLATE CREAM COOKIES

Prepare Vanilla Cream Cookie recipe and:
       add 2 tablespoons cocoa, sifted
       increase sugar to 1 cup
       omit cream of tartar

Prepare Cream Filling recipe as directed.

LEMON CREAM COOKIES

Prepare Vanilla Cream Cookie recipe and:
       omit cream of tartar
       replace vanilla with 1 teaspoon lemon extract
       replace 2 tablespoons of water with lemon juice
       add 1/8 teaspoon yellow food color (optional)

Prepare Cream Filling recipe and:
       replace vanilla with 1 teaspoon lemon extract

JELLY ROLL COOKIES

1 1/2 cups Gluten-free Cookie Flour Mix (see page 80)
1/2 teaspoon xanthan gum
1 teaspoon Egg Replacer™
1/4 teaspoon baking soda
1/4 teaspoon salt
1/4 cup sugar
1/4 cup brown sugar
1/4 cup margarine
1/4 cup shortening
1/2 teaspoon vanilla
2 to 3 tablespoons milk (rice, soy, or cow)
Fruit preserves, slightly warmed to thin out

Preheat oven to 375°F. Cover a cookie sheet with parchment paper.

Combine dry ingredients, except sugars, in a bowl and set aside. In another bowl, beat margarine and shortening with an electric mixer until blended. Then add sugars and beat until creamy. Add vanilla and milk. Add dry ingredients. If dough is too dry, add just enough milk to form a sticky ball. Divide the dough in half.

Roll out the dough into a 1/4" thick rectangle between two sheets of wax paper dusted with tapioca flour. Spread a thin layer of fruit preserves onto the dough. Roll dough up to form a log. Wrap in wax paper and chill 30 minutes in the freezer. Cut into 1/4" disks and place on the prepared cookie sheet. Bake 10 to 12 minutes. Cool on pan for 1 minute and transfer to cooling rack.

Makes 2 1/2 dozen.

CINNAMON ROLL COOKIES

Prepare cookie dough as directed above. Sprinkle dough with cinnamon sugar and a dash of nutmeg. Roll into a log and bake as directed.

PRESS COOKIES

1 1/2 cups Gluten-free Cookie Flour Mix (see page 80)
1/8 teaspoon xanthan gum
3/4 teaspoon Egg Replacer™
1/8 teaspoon baking powder
1/8 teaspoon salt
1/2 cup sugar
1/2 cup margarine
1 teaspoon vanilla
1 tablespoon water
*can be tinted with food coloring if desired

Preheat oven to 350°F.

Combine dry ingredients in a bowl and set aside. In another bowl, beat margarine and sugar with an electric mixer until creamy. Add water, vanilla and food coloring (if desired). Add dry ingredients.

Use a cookie press to form the cookies or use a 1" melon baller to measure each cookie. Drop onto ungreased cookie sheet about 1" apart. Bake 8-9 minutes. Cool on pan for 2 minutes and then transfer to cooling rack.

Makes 2 1/2 dozen.

LEMON PRESS COOKIES

Follow directions above and substitute 1 teaspoon lemon extract for vanilla.

SPICE PRESS COOKIES

Follow directions above and add 1/2 teaspoon cinnamon and 1/8 teaspoon nutmeg to dry ingredients.

FUDGE BROWNIES

1 1/2 cups Gluten-free Cookie Flour Mix (see page 80)
1/2 teaspoon xanthan gum
1 tablespoon Egg Replacer™
2 teaspoons baking powder
1/2 teaspoon salt
1 1/4 cups sugar
1/2 cup margarine
1 teaspoon vanilla
1 1/4 cups milk (rice, soy, or cow)
3 ounces unsweetened chocolate, melted and cooled

Icing:
3 tablespoons margarine
2 ounces unsweetened chocolate
1/4 cup milk (rice, soy, or cow)
3 cups confectioners' sugar

Preheat oven to 350°F. Line the bottom and sides of an 8"x8" pan with parchment paper. Leave some paper hanging over sides of pan to allow easy removal of brownies after baking.

For brownies: Combine dry ingredients, except sugar, in a bowl and set aside. In another bowl, beat margarine and sugar with an electric mixer until creamy. Add vanilla and chocolate. Then alternate adding milk and dry ingredients. Pour into the prepared pan and bake for 20 to 25 minutes or until toothpick inserted in center comes out clean.

For icing: Combine margarine and chocolate in a small sauce pot. Stir on medium low heat until melted. Add confectioners' sugar and enough milk to make it a good spreading consistency.

Spread icing over brownies and cool thoroughly in pan. Carefully remove by lifting up exposed parchment paper. Cut into 2" squares.

Makes 16 bars.

GRANOLA BARS

This recipe is not gluten-free.

1/4 cup brown rice flour
1/4 cup potato starch
1/4 cup oat flour
1/4 cup sweet white rice flour
1/2 teaspoon xanthan gum
1 teaspoon baking powder
1 teaspoon cinnamon
1/3 cup sugar
1 cup brown sugar
6 tablespoons margarine
2 teaspoons light corn syrup
1 teaspoon vanilla
1 1/2 cups oats
1 cup crispy rice cereal
1/2 cup semi-sweet chocolate chips
1/2 cup dried fruit (diced apples, raisins, chopped cranberries)

Preheat oven to 350°F. Line the bottom and sides of a 13"x9" pan with parchment paper.

Combine flours, xanthan gum, baking powder, and cinnamon in a bowl and set aside. In another bowl, beat margarine and sugars with an electric mixer until creamy. Add corn syrup and vanilla. Add flour mixture and mix well. By hand, stir in remaining ingredients (oats, cereal, chips, and fruit) until thoroughly mixed. Press into the prepared pan. Bake 20 minutes. Cool thoroughly in pan. Cut into 2" squares.

Makes 24 bars.

COMMENTS

CHAPTER 8

CAKES and ICINGS

The cakes in this chapter are wonderfully moist and light, and the "buttercream" icing is perfect for both icing and decorating cakes.

The liquid amounts may need to be adjusted for high altitudes or even weather. If there is a dimple in the center of the cake, reduce the liquid slightly the next time you use that recipe.

WHITE CAKE

1 1/2 cups brown rice flour
1/2 cup potato starch
1/4 cup tapioca flour
3/4 teaspoon xanthan gum
1 tablespoon Egg Replacer™
1 teaspoon baking powder
1/2 teaspoon baking soda
1/2 teaspoon cream of tartar
1/2 teaspoon salt
1 1/2 cups sugar
1/2 cup canola oil
2 teaspoons vanilla
1/2 cup warm milk (rice, soy, or cow)
2 tablespoons applesauce
"Buttercream" icing (see page 104) *or*
Vanilla glaze (see page 105)

Preheat oven to 375° F. Line 2 6" round cake pans with parchment paper. Grease paper and sides of pan.

Combine all dry ingredients in a bowl. In another bowl, combine oil, vanilla, applesauce, and warm milk. Add milk mixture to dry ingredients and stir thoroughly until batter is smooth. Fill pans and bake 30 to 35 minutes or until wooden toothpick inserted in center comes out clean. Cool in pan 20 minutes, and then transfer to rack to cool completely. Cover with "Buttercream" icing or drizzle with vanilla glaze as desired.

SPICE CAKE

1 1/2 cups brown rice flour
1/2 cup potato starch
1/4 cup tapioca flour
3/4 teaspoon xanthan gum
1 tablespoon Egg Replacer™
1 teaspoon baking powder
1/2 teaspoon baking soda
1/2 teaspoon cream of tartar
1/2 teaspoon salt
1 teaspoon cinnamon
1/4 teaspoon nutmeg
1/8 teaspoon allspice
1 1/2 cups sugar
1/2 cup canola oil
2 teaspoons vanilla
1/2 cup warm milk (rice, soy, or cow)
2 tablespoons applesauce
"Buttercream" icing (see page 104) *or*
Vanilla glaze (see page 105)

Preheat oven to 375° F. Line 2 6" round cake pans with parchment paper. Grease paper and sides of pan.

Combine all dry ingredients in a bowl. In another bowl, combine oil, vanilla, applesauce, and warm milk. Add milk mixture to dry ingredients and stir thoroughly until batter is smooth. Fill pans and bake 30 to 35 minutes or until wooden toothpick inserted in center comes out clean. Cool in pan 20 minutes, and then transfer to rack to cool completely. Cover with "Buttercream" icing or drizzle with vanilla glaze as desired.

CARROT CAKE

1 1/2 cups brown rice flour
1/2 cup potato starch
1/4 cup tapioca flour
3/4 teaspoon xanthan gum
1 tablespoon Egg Replacer™
1 teaspoon baking powder
1/2 teaspoon baking soda
1/2 teaspoon cream of tartar
1/2 teaspoon salt
1 teaspoon cinnamon
1/4 teaspoon nutmeg
1/8 teaspoon allspice
1 1/2 cups sugar
1/2 cup canola oil
2 teaspoons vanilla
1/2 cup warm milk (rice, soy, or cow)
2 tablespoons applesauce
1/2 cup grated carrots
"Buttercream" icing (see page 104) *or*
Vanilla glaze (see page 105)

Preheat oven to 375° F. Line 2 6" round cake pans with parchment paper. Grease paper and sides of pan.

Combine all dry ingredients in a bowl. In another bowl, combine oil, vanilla, applesauce, and warm milk. Add milk mixture to dry ingredients and stir thoroughly until batter is smooth. Stir in carrots by hand. Fill pans and bake 30 to 35 minutes or until wooden pick inserted in center comes out clean. Cool in pan 20 minutes, and then transfer to rack to cool completely. Cover with "Buttercream" icing or drizzle with vanilla glaze as desired.

CHOCOLATE CAKE

1 1/2 cups brown rice flour
1/2 cup potato starch
1/4 cup tapioca flour
1/8 cup cocoa, sifted
3/4 teaspoon xanthan gum
1 tablespoon Egg Replacer™
1 teaspoon baking powder
1/2 teaspoon soda
1/4 teaspoon salt
1 1/2 cups sugar
1/4 cup canola oil
2 teaspoon vanilla
3/4 cup milk (rice, soy, or cow)
2 tablespoons applesauce
Chocolate "Buttercream" Icing (see page 104)

Preheat oven to 375° F. Line 2 6" round cake pans with parchment paper. Grease paper and sides of pan.

Combine all dry ingredients in a bowl, making sure to sift cocoa well (to minimize lumps of cocoa). In another bowl, combine oil, vanilla, applesauce, and milk. Add milk mixture to dry ingredients and stir thoroughly until batter is smooth. Fill pans and bake 30 to 35 minutes or until wooden toothpick inserted in center comes out clean. Cool in pan 20 minutes, and then transfer to rack to cool completely. Cover with Chocolate "Buttercream" Icing as desired.

DOUBLE CHOCOLATE CHIP CAKE

Follow recipe as above and stir in 1/2 cup semi-sweet chocolate chips to batter. Bake as directed.

ORANGE CAKE

2/3 cup brown rice flour
2/3 cup potato starch
2/3 cup tapioca flour
1 teaspoon xanthan gum
2 teaspoons Egg Replacer™
1 1/2 teaspoons baking powder
1/2 teaspoon baking soda
1/2 teaspoon salt
1 1/4 cups sugar
1/4 cup oil (canola or soy)
2 tablespoons applesauce
3/4 cup orange juice (preferably fresh squeezed)
1 1/2 teaspoons orange zest
Orange glaze (see page 105)

Preheat oven to 375° F. Line 2 6" round cake pans with parchment paper. Grease paper and sides of pan.

Combine all dry ingredients in a bowl. In another bowl, combine oil, applesauce, orange zest, and orange juice. Add juice mixture to dry ingredients and stir thoroughly until batter is smooth. Fill pans and bake 30 to 35 minutes or until wooden toothpick inserted in center comes out clean. Cool in pan 20 minutes, and then transfer to rack to cool completely. Drizzle with orange glaze as desired.

LEMON CAKE

2/3 cup brown rice flour
2/3 cup potato starch
2/3 cup tapioca flour
1 teaspoon xanthan gum
2 teaspoons Egg Replacer™
1 1/2 teaspoons baking powder
1/2 teaspoon baking soda
1/2 teaspoon salt
1 1/4 cups sugar
1/4 cup oil (canola or soy)
2 tablespoons applesauce
3/4 cup lemon juice (fresh squeezed)
1 1/2 teaspoons lemon zest
Lemon glaze (see page 105)

Preheat oven to 375° F. Line 2 6" round cake pans with parchment paper. Grease paper and sides of pan.

Combine all dry ingredients in a bowl. In another bowl, combine oil, applesauce, lemon zest, and lemon juice. Add juice mixture to dry ingredients and stir thoroughly until batter is smooth. Fill pans and bake 30 to 35 minutes or until wooden toothpick inserted in center comes out clean. Cool in pan 20 minutes, and then transfer to rack to cool completely. Drizzle with lemon glaze as desired.

"BUTTERCREAM" ICING

1 cup shortening
4 tablespoons water
1 teaspoon vanilla
1/4 teaspoon salt
1 pound confectioners' sugar

Dissolve salt and vanilla in water and set aside. Use an electric mixer to beat shortening for 1 minute. Add water mixture slowly until mixed. Add sugar in small batches until all the sugar is combined. If icing is too stiff, add just enough water until icing is smooth enough to spread.

CHOCOLATE "BUTTERCREAM" ICING

Follow directions as above, except add 2 ounces of melted unsweetened chocolate before adding confectioners' sugar.

ORANGE GLAZE or LEMON GLAZE

1 cup confectioners' sugar
orange juice *or* lemon juice
1 teaspoon light corn syrup

Combine confectioners' sugar and enough juice to make glaze consistency (about 2 to 4 teaspoons). Then add corn syrup. Drizzle onto cake.

VANILLA GLAZE

1 cup confectioners' sugar
milk (rice, soy, cow) or water
1/4 teaspoon vanilla
1 teaspoon light corn syrup

Combine confectioners' sugar, vanilla and enough milk to make glaze consistency (about 2 to 4 teaspoons). Then add corn syrup. Drizzle onto cake.

COMMENTS

CHAPTER 9
OTHER DESSERTS

Pie Crust
"Graham" Cracker Crust
Sweet Potato Pie
Apple Pie
Peach Pie
Cherry Pie
Refrigerated Blueberry Pie
Gluten-free Crisp Topping
Oatmeal Crisp Topping
Apple Crisp
Peach Crisp
Biscuit Cobbler Topping
Lattice Cobbler Topping
Apple Cobbler
Peach Cobbler
Cherry Raspberry Cobbler
Blueberry Raspberry Cobbler
Fruit Tarts
Cinnamon Rolls
Apple Fritters
Doughnuts
Chocolate Doughnuts
Glazes for Doughnuts

PIE CRUST

1/2 cup brown rice flour or barley flour (if gluten is permitted)
1/2 cup tapioca flour
1/4 cup sweet white rice flour
1/2 teaspoon xanthan gum
1 tablespoon sugar
1/4 teaspoon salt
1/3 cup shortening
4 tablespoons cold water

Combine dry ingredients in a bowl. Use a fork or pastry cutter to cut shortening into flour mixture. Add just enough cold water to form smooth ball. Roll out crust between two sheets of wax paper, lightly dusted with flour. Carefully transfer into pie pan.

If pre-baking is required, use a fork to prick holes in the bottom of the crust to prevent the crust from rising. Bake at 400°F for 10 minutes.

"GRAHAM" CRACKER CRUST

2 cups finely crushed "Graham Crackers" (see page 64)
1/4 cup sugar
7 tablespoons melted margarine

Combine all ingredients. Press mixture firmly into a 9" pie pan.

Bake at 350°F for 8 to 10 minutes, until edges begin to lightly brown. Let crust cool completely before filling.

SWEET POTATO PIE

2 large sweet potatoes, baked
3/8 cup brown sugar
1/2 teaspoon cinnamon
1/8 teaspoon allspice
1/8 teaspoon nutmeg
1/4 teaspoon vanilla
1 tablespoon margarine
1 to 2 tablespoons milk (rice, soy, or cow)
1 teaspoon unflavored gelatin or Agar powder
1 pie crust, unbaked (see page 108)

Preheat oven to 400° F.

Prepare pie crust and place into 8" or 9" pie pan.

Combine all ingredients in a bowl and beat with an electric mixer until creamy. Fill pie crust and bake for 30 minutes.

For baked sweet potatoes:
Preheat oven to 400° F. Wash potatoes and wrap in foil. Bake on a cookie sheet until soft, about 2 hours. (Cover the pan with foil for easy clean-up, since sweet potatoes will spill sugar that burns on the pan.) Remove cooked sweet potatoes from the skins and place in a bowl.

*Tip: To minimize strings in baked sweet potatoes, remove whole sweet potato from skin after cooked. With sharp paring knife, make cross-sectional cuts across the whole potato (as if cutting disks) as close together as possible. This will decrease the size of the strings so that they will not be noticed when eaten.

APPLE PIE

6 cups baking apples, peeled, and thinly sliced (about 3 large apples)
1 tablespoon lemon juice
1/2 cup sugar
1/4 cup tapioca flour
1 teaspoon cinnamon
1/8 teaspoon nutmeg
1/4 teaspoon salt
1 tablespoon margarine
2 pie crusts, unbaked (see page 108)

Preheat oven to 400°F.

Prepare two pie crusts. Place one crust into 8" or 9" pie pan. Set second crust aside.

Combine dry ingredients in small bowl. In a large bowl, toss apples with lemon juice and add dry ingredients. Fill pie crust with apple mixture and dot with margarine. Cover with second crust. Crimp edges and poke holes in top crust to vent steam. Bake for 40 to 45 minutes, or until crust is golden and apples are tender. If edges brown too quickly, wrap edges with foil.

PEACH PIE

6 cups sliced peaches, fresh or frozen, and thawed
2 tablespoons lemon juice
3/4 cup sugar
1/4 cup tapioca flour
1/2 teaspoon cinnamon
1/4 teaspoon nutmeg
2 tablespoons margarine
2 pie crusts, unbaked (see page 108)

Preheat oven to 400°F.

Prepare two pie crusts. Place one crust into 8" or 9" pie pan. Set second crust aside.

Combine dry ingredients in a small bowl. In large bowl, toss peaches with lemon juice and add dry ingredients. Fill pie crust with peach mixture and dot with margarine. Cover with second crust. Crimp edges and poke holes in top crust to vent steam. Bake for 30 to 40 minutes, or until crust is golden and peaches are tender. If edges brown too quickly, wrap edges with foil.

CHERRY PIE

6 cups pitted, tart red cherries, frozen and thawed
1 cup sugar
1/4 cup tapioca flour
1/8 teaspoon salt
1 tablespoon margarine
2 pie crusts, unbaked (see page 108)

Preheat oven to 400°F.

Prepare two pie crusts. Place one crust into 8" or 9" pie pan. Set second crust aside.

Combine dry ingredients in a large bowl and toss in cherries. Fill pie crust with cherry mixture and dot with margarine. Cover with second crust. Crimp edges and poke holes in top crust to vent steam. Bake for 35 to 40 minutes, or until crust is golden and cherries are tender. If edges brown too quickly, wrap edges with foil.

REFRIGERATED BLUEBERRY PIE

4 cups blueberries, fresh or frozen and thawed
1/2 cup water, divided
1 cup sugar
1/3 cup tapioca flour
1 pie crusts, pre-baked (see page 108)

Preheat oven to 400°F.

Prepare pie crust and place into 8" or 9" pie pan. Use a fork to prick holes in the crust and bake 10 minutes. Cool completely.

Boil 1 cup blueberries, sugar, and 1/4 cup water. Make a paste of tapioca flour and 1/4 cup water. Add to boiling blueberries. Stir until thickened. Cool and add remaining blueberries. Pour into pie shell and refrigerate until firm.

GLUTEN-FREE CRISP TOPPING

1/4 cup brown rice flour
1/4 cup potato starch
1/4 cup tapioca flour
1/4 cup sweet white rice flour
1/4 teaspoon xanthan gum
1/8 teaspoon salt
1/2 teaspoon cinnamon
1/2 cup brown sugar
2 tablespoons margarine

Combine dry ingredients in a bowl. Use a fork or pastry cutter to cut margarine into dry ingredients to form course crumbs. Pour on top of fruit filling and gently pat down.

Bake for 30 to 40 minutes at 400°F.

OATMEAL CRISP TOPPING

This recipe is not gluten-free.

1/2 cup oats
1/8 cup brown rice flour
1/8 cup potato starch
1/8 cup tapioca flour
1/8 cup sweet white rice flour
1 tablespoon oat flour
1/4 teaspoon xanthan gum
1/4 teaspoon salt
1/2 teaspoon cinnamon
1/2 cup brown sugar
2 tablespoons margarine

Combine dry ingredients in a bowl. Use a fork or pastry cutter to cut margarine into dry ingredients to form course crumbs. Pour on top of fruit filling and gently pat down.

Bake for 30 to 40 minutes at 400°F.

APPLE CRISP

6 cups sliced baking apples
1 tablespoon lemon juice
1/4 cup tapioca flour
1 teaspoon cinnamon
1/8 teaspoon nutmeg
2 tablespoons sugar
Gluten-Free Crisp topping (see page 115) *or*
Oatmeal Crisp topping recipe (see page 116)

Preheat oven to 400°F.

Combine dry ingredients in a small bowl. In a large bowl, toss apples with lemon juice and add dry ingredients. Pour into an 8"x8" baking dish. Cover with crisp topping of choice and gently pat down. Place dish onto cookie sheet to catch spills and bake for 30 to 40 minutes. If topping gets too brown, loosely cover with foil for last 10 minutes of baking.

PEACH CRISP

4 cups sliced peaches, fresh or frozen, and thawed
1 tablespoon lemon juice
1/4 cup tapioca flour
1 teaspoon cinnamon
1/8 teaspoon nutmeg
2 tablespoons sugar
Gluten-Free Crisp topping (see page 115) *or*
Oatmeal Crisp topping recipe (see page 116)

Preheat oven to 400°F.

Combine dry ingredients in a small bowl. In a large bowl, toss peaches with lemon juice and add dry ingredients. Pour into an 8"x8" baking dish. Cover with crisp recipe of choice and gently pat down. Place dish onto cookie sheet to catch spills and bake for 30 to 40 minutes. If topping gets too brown, loosely cover with foil for last 10 minutes of baking.

BISCUIT COBBLER TOPPING

1/4 cup brown rice flour
1/4 cup potato starch
1/4 cup tapioca flour
1/4 cup sweet white rice flour
1/4 teaspoon xanthan gum
1 1/2 teaspoons Egg Replacer™
1 1/2 teaspoons baking powder
1/4 teaspoon salt
2 tablespoons sugar
1/4 cup margarine
1/4 cup milk (rice, soy, or cow)

Combine dry ingredients in a bowl. Use a fork or pastry cutter to cut margarine into dry ingredients. Stir in milk with a fork to form a loose ball. Spread topping onto fruit cobbler of choice.

Bake for 30 to 40 minutes at 400°F.

LATTICE COBBLER TOPPING

1/2 cup brown rice flour
1/2 cup potato starch
1/4 cup tapioca flour
1/4 cup sweet white rice flour
1/2 teaspoon xanthan gum
1 tablespoon Egg Replacer™
2 teaspoons baking powder
1/4 teaspoon salt
2 tablespoons sugar
1/4 cup margarine
1/2 cup milk (rice, soy, or cow)

Combine dry ingredients in a bowl. Use a fork or pastry cutter to cut margarine into dry ingredients. Stir in milk with a fork to form smooth ball. Roll out dough to 1/8" thick onto wax paper, lightly dusted with tapioca starch.

For Lattice: Use pizza cutter to cut out 10" strips. Carefully transfer strips onto fruit cobbler filling by laying strips down in one direction, leaving a small gap between each strip, and then laying more strips across the first strips. Bake for 30 to 40 minutes at 400°F.

For shapes: Use biscuit or cookie cutter to cut out enough shapes to nearly cover fruit cobbler filling. Leave gap between each shape for filling to bubble up. Bake for 30 to 40 minutes at 400°F.

For tarts: Transfer dough to tart pan. Bake for 10 to 15 minutes at 400°F.

APPLE COBBLER

6 cups baking apples, peeled and sliced (about 3 large apples)
1 tablespoon lemon juice
1/4 cup water
1/2 cup sugar
1/4 cup tapioca flour
1 teaspoon cinnamon
1/8 teaspoon nutmeg
1/4 teaspoon salt
Biscuit Cobbler Topping recipe (see page 119) *or*
Lattice Cobbler Topping recipe (see page 120)

Preheat oven to 400°F.

Combine dry ingredients and water in sauce pot. Cook over medium low heat until thickened and bubbly. Add margarine, lemon juice, and apples. Pour into 9" baking dish. Cover with cobbler topping of choice. Place dish onto cookie sheet to catch spills and bake for 30 to 40 minutes. If topping gets too brown, loosely cover with foil for last 10 minutes of baking.

PEACH COBBLER

4 cups sliced peaches, fresh or frozen, and thawed
1/2 cup water
1 tablespoon lemon juice
1/2 cup brown sugar
2 tablespoons tapioca flour
1 teaspoon cinnamon
1/4 teaspoon nutmeg
1 tablespoon margarine
Biscuit Cobbler Topping recipe (page 119) *or*
Lattice Cobbler Topping recipe (page 120)

Preheat oven to 400°F.

Combine dry ingredients and water in sauce pot. Cook over medium low heat until thickened and bubbly. Add margarine, lemon juice, and peaches. Pour into 9" baking dish. Cover with cobbler topping of choice. Place dish onto cookie sheet to catch spills and bake for 30 to 40 minutes. If topping gets too brown, loosely cover with foil for last 10 minutes of baking.

CHERRY RASPBERRY COBBLER

2 cups pitted, tart red cherries, frozen and thawed
2 cups red raspberries, frozen and thawed
1/2 cup water
1/2 cup sugar
2 tablespoons tapioca flour
Biscuit Cobbler Topping recipe (page 119) *or*
Lattice Cobbler Topping recipe (page 120)

Preheat oven to 400°F.

Combine dry ingredients, water, and cherries in sauce pot. Cook over medium low heat until thickened and bubbly. Stir in cherries and raspberries. Pour into 9" baking dish. Cover with cobbler topping of choice. Place dish onto cookie sheet to catch spills and bake for 30 to 40 minutes. If topping gets too brown, loosely cover with foil for last 10 minutes of baking.

BLUEBERRY RASPBERRY COBBLER

3 cups blueberries, frozen and thawed
1 cup red raspberries, frozen and thawed
1/2 cup water
1/2 cup sugar
2 tablespoons tapioca flour
Biscuit Cobbler Topping recipe (page 119) *or*
Lattice Cobbler Topping recipe (page 120)

Preheat oven to 400°F.

Combine dry ingredients, water, and 1 cup blueberries in sauce pot. Cook over medium low heat until thickened and bubbly. Stir in raspberries and remaining blueberries. Pour into 9" baking dish. Cover with cobbler topping recipe of choice. Place dish onto cookie sheet to catch spills and bake for 30 to 40 minutes. If topping gets too brown, loosely cover with foil for last 10 minutes of baking.

FRUIT TARTS

Lattice Cobbler Topping recipe (see page 120)
fresh fruit of choice:
  apples, strawberries, blueberries, raspberries, blackberries, cherries, plums, kiwi, oranges

Preheat oven to 400°F.

Prepare Lattice Cobbler Topping. Press dough into tart pans or mini-tart pans. Use a fork to prick holes in the dough to prevent the dough from rising. Bake for 10 to 15 minutes or crust is lightly browned. Cool tart crusts completely.

Fill the tart crusts with fresh fruits. Fruits can be brushed with corn syrup thinned with water to add shine and keep fruits looking their best for serving. Serve immediately.

CINNAMON ROLLS

1 cup brown rice flour
1 cup potato starch
1/2 cup tapioca flour
1/2 teaspoon Dough Enhancer™*
2 teaspoons xanthan gum
1 1/2 teaspoons Egg Replacer™
1/2 teaspoon salt
1/4 cup sugar
1/4 cup margarine
1/2 cup hot milk (rice, soy, or cow)
1 package yeast
1/4 cup water, warm

Preheat oven to 350° F. Prepare baking sheet lined with parchment paper.

In a small bowl, dissolve yeast in warm water. Combine flours, xanthan gum, and Egg Replacer™ in a bowl and set aside. In another bowl, combine margarine, sugar, salt, and hot milk. Mix well and cool slightly.

Combine all wet ingredients in mixing bowl and mix thoroughly. Gradually stir in flour mixture until dough forms a ball. Gently knead dough into smooth ball. Place back in bowl and cover with damp towel. Let rise for 30 minutes.

Divide dough in quarters. Keep unused portions covered. Lightly cover surface with tapioca or potato starch. Use fingers to gently press out dough into rectangle. Spread dough with thin amount of margarine and sprinkle generously with cinnamon sugar. Carefully roll dough into a log. Cut rolls 1" thick and place on baking sheet. Bake for 15 minutes or lightly browned. Repeat for remaining dough.

*Note: Dough Enhancer contains soy lecithin. If you are avoiding soy lecithin, then omit from the recipe. The texture of the dough will not be quite as smooth as with it; however, the taste will be just as good.

APPLE FRITTERS

1/4 cup brown rice flour
1/4 cup potato starch
1/4 cup tapioca flour
1/8 cup oat flour or sorghum flour (for gluten-free)
1/8 cup sweet white rice flour
1/2 teaspoon xanthan gum
1 1/2 teaspoons Egg Replacer™
1 1/2 teaspoons baking powder
1/4 teaspoon salt
3 tablespoons sugar
1/2 to 3/4 cup milk (rice, soy, or cow)
1 baking apple, cut into cubes
oil for frying

Fill a small sauce pot with oil about 2" deep. Preheat oil to 360° F using frying thermometer. Leave the thermometer in place during cooking.

Combine dry ingredients in a bowl. Add just enough milk to make smooth but thick batter. Dip apples into batter, completely coating entire surface. Carefully drop fritters into hot oil. Cook until deep golden brown on both sides, about 1 minute. Remove from oil and drain on paper towel. Dust with confectioners' sugar and serve hot.

Note: Be sure to keep oil temperature around 360°F. If the oil gets too hot, the outside of the fritters will cook too fast, leaving raw dough on the inside. If the oil gets too cool, the fritters will absorb the oil and will taste greasy.

DOUGHNUTS

1/2 cup brown rice flour
1/2 cup potato starch
1/4 cup tapioca flour
1/4 cup oat flour or sorghum flour (for gluten-free)
1/8 cup sweet white rice flour
3/4 teaspoon xanthan gum
1 1/2 teaspoons Egg Replacer™
1 teaspoon baking powder
1/4 teaspoon salt
1/4 teaspoon cinnamon
1/8 teaspoon nutmeg
1/3 cup sugar
2 tablespoons margarine, melted
1/4 cup milk (rice, soy, or cow)
1 teaspoon vanilla
oil for frying
Chocolate Glaze *or*
Vanilla Glaze (see page 129)

Fill oil about 2" deep in a 1 or 2-quart pot. Preheat oil to 360° F using frying thermometer. Leave the thermometer in place during cooking.

Combine dry ingredients in a bowl. Add melted margarine, vanilla, and just enough milk to form a stiff dough. Wrap dough in wax paper and chill in the freezer for 30 minutes. Cover wax paper with potato starch and roll out dough to 1/2" thick. Cut with doughnut cutter.

Carefully drop doughnuts and doughnut holes into hot oil. Cook one at a time until deep golden brown on both sides, about 1 minute. Remove from oil, drain on a paper towel, and cool.

After completely cooled, sprinkle with confectioners' sugar or dip doughnuts into chocolate or vanilla glaze.

Makes 8 doughnuts and 8 doughnut holes.

CHOCOLATE DOUGHNUTS

Prepare Doughnut recipe and
    add 1 tablespoon cocoa, sifted
    increase sugar to 1/2 cup

CHOCOLATE GLAZE for DOUGHNUTS

1 cup confectioner's sugar
1 ounce unsweetened chocolate, melted
1 tablespoon margarine, melted
boiling water

Combine sugar, melted chocolate, margarine, and enough boiling water to make drizzling consistency.

VANILLA GLAZE for DOUGHNUTS

1 cup confectioners' sugar
1 tablespoon light corn syrup
1/2 teaspoon vanilla
milk (rice, soy, or cow)

Combine sugar, corn syrup, vanilla, and enough milk to make drizzling consistency.

COMMENTS

CHAPTER 10
COLD TREATS, SAUCES, and BEVERAGES

Fruit Sorbet
Gelatin Squares
Carbonated Fruit Drinks
Fruit Sauces

FRUIT SORBET

1 can frozen juice concentrate
1 1/2 cups boiling water
1 1/4 teaspoons xanthan gum
2 tablespoons sugar

Combine all ingredients in blender and puree for 2 minutes. Pour into containers and freeze until firm.

GELATIN SQUARES

1 package unflavored gelatin
1/2 cup boiling fruit juice
1 cup cold fruit juice

Dissolve gelatin in boiling fruit juice. Add cold juice and stir to completely mix. Pour into glass container(s) and refrigerate until firm. Cut into squares when ready to serve.

CARBONATED FRUIT DRINKS

1 can frozen juice concentrate
club soda (carbonated water)

Prepare juice concentrate according to directions on can, except substitute club soda for water.

FRUIT SAUCES

Note: Sauces will thicken after cooling. However, if a thicker sauce is preferred, in a separate bowl thoroughly mix a small amount of hot liquid with 1/2 teaspoon tapioca flour. Add this mixture to the cooking fruit sauce. Never add any flour to the hot sauce all at once, because the flour will clump together and will not evenly mix.

Strawberry, Blueberry, Cherry, Raspberry, or Peach:
1 cup fruit, fresh or frozen (thawed and drained)
1/4 cup water or apple juice
2 tablespoons sugar
1 tablespoon tapioca flour

Combine tapioca flour, sugar, and juice or water in small sauce pot over medium heat. Whisk constantly to thoroughly combine. Gently boil until thickened and bubbly. Add fruit and stir gently for 1 minute. Remove from heat and cool.

Makes about 1 cup of sauce.

Pineapple:
1 cup canned crushed pineapple in own juice (drain and reserve liquid)
1/4 cup reserved liquid
1 tablespoons sugar
1 tablespoon tapioca flour

Combine tapioca flour, sugar, and juice in small sauce pot over medium heat. Whisk constantly to thoroughly combine. Gently boil until thickened and bubbly. Add fruit and stir gently for 1 minute. Remove from heat and cool.

Makes about 1 cup of sauce.

FRUIT SAUCES (continued)

Apple:
1 cup cooking apple, diced
1/4 cup water
2 tablespoons sugar
1 tablespoon tapioca flour
1/2 teaspoon fresh lemon juice (optional)
1/8 teaspoon cinnamon (optional)

Combine apples, sugar, cinnamon, water, and lemon juice in small sauce pot over medium heat. Gently boil until apples are tender. In separate bowl, combine tapioca flour with enough hot liquid from apples to thoroughly dissolve flour. Add flour mixture to apples and stir until thickened and bubbly. Remove from heat and cool.

Makes about 1 cup of sauce.

COMMENTS

CHAPTER 11
HOW TO READ LABELS

Wheat-Free Diet
Egg-Free Diet
Soy-Free Diet
Milk-Free Diet
Peanut-Free Diet
Tree Nut-Free Diet
Gluten-Free Diet

HOW TO READ LABELS

Note: The information for wheat, eggs, milk, peanuts, tree nuts, and soy appears with permission from the Food Allergy & Anaphylaxis Network, 2003. This information is continuously being updated, so obtain the most recent information from FAAN directly (see page 146).

HOW TO READ A LABEL for a WHEAT-FREE DIET	
Avoid foods that contain wheat or any of these ingredients:	pasta seitan semolina spelt vital gluten wheat (*bran, germ, gluten, malt*) whole wheat berries
bran bread crumbs bulgur couscous cracker meal durum farina flour (*all purpose, bread, durum, cake, enriched, graham, high gluten, high protein, instant, pastry, self-rising, soft wheat, steel ground, stone ground, whole wheat*) gluten kamut matzoh, matzoh meal (*also spelled as matzo*)	*May indicate the presence of wheat protein:* flavoring (including natural and artificial) hydrolyzed protein soy sauce starch (gelatinized starch, modified starch, modified food starch, vegetable starch, wheat starch) surimi

Printed with permission from the Food Allergy & Anaphylaxis Network, 2003

HOW TO READ A LABEL for an EGG-FREE DIET *Avoid foods that contain eggs or any of these ingredients:* albumin (*also spelled as albumen*) egg (*dried, powdered, solids, white, yolk*) eggnog lysozyme (*used in Europe*) mayonnaise meringue (*meringue powder*) surimi	*May indicate the presence of egg protein:* flavoring (*including natural and artificial*) lecithin macaroni marzipan marshmallows nougat pasta

Printed with permission from the Food Allergy & Anaphylaxis Network, 2003

HOW TO READ A LABEL for a SOY-FREE DIET *Avoid foods that contain soy or any of these ingredients:* edamame hydrolyzed soy protein miso natto shoyu sauce soy (*soy albumin, soy fiber, soy flour, soy grits, soy milk, soy nuts, soy sprouts*) soya soybean (*curd, granules*) soy protein (*concentrate, isolate*) soy sauce Tamari	Tempeh textured vegetable protein (TVP) tofu *May indicate the presence of soy protein:* flavoring (*including natural and artificial*) vegetable broth vegetable gum vegetable starch • Studies show most individuals allergic to soy may safely eat soy lecithin and soybean oil.

Printed with permission from the Food Allergy & Anaphylaxis Network, 2003

HOW TO READ A LABEL for a MILK-FREE DIET

Avoid foods that contain milk or any of these ingredients:

artificial butter flavor
butter, butter fat, butter oil
buttermilk
casein (*casein hydrolysate*)
caseinates (*in all forms*)
cheese
cream
cottage cheese
curds
custard
ghee
half & half®
lactalbumin, lactalbumin phosphate
lactulose
milk (*in all forms including condensed, derivative, dry, evaporated, goat's milk, and milk from other animals, low-fat, malted, milkfat, non-fat, powder, protein, skimmed, solids, whole*)

nougat
pudding
rennet casein
sour cream, sour cream solids
sour milk solids
whey (*in all forms*)
yogurt

May indicate the presence of milk protein:

caramel candies
chocolate
flavorings (*including natural and artificial*)
high protein flour
lactic acid starter culture
lactose
luncheon meat, hotdogs, sausages
margarine
non-dairy products

Printed with permission from the Food Allergy & Anaphylaxis Network, 2003

**HOW TO READ A LABEL
for a PEANUT-FREE DIET**
*Avoid foods that contain
peanuts or any of these
ingredients:*

artificial nuts
beer nuts
cold pressed, expelled, or
   extruded peanut oil
goobers
ground nuts
mandelonas
mixed nuts
monkey nuts
nutmeat
nut pieces
peanut
peanut butter
peanut flour

*May indicate the presence of
   peanut protein:*

African, Chinese, Indonesian,
   Mexican, Thai, and
   Vietnamese dishes
baked goods (*pastries, cookies,
   etc.*)
candy (*including chocolate
   candy*)
chili
egg rolls
enchilada sauce

flavoring (*including natural and
   artificial*)
marzipan
nougat

• Studies show that most allergic
  individuals can safely eat peanut
  oil (***not*** cold pressed, expelled,
  or extruded peanut oil).

• Arachis oil is peanut oil

• Experts advise patients allergic
  to peanuts to avoid tree nuts as
  well.

• A study showed that unlike
  other legumes, there is a strong
  possibility of cross reactions
  between peanuts and lupine.

• Sunflower seeds are often
  produced on equipment shared
  with peanuts.

*Printed with permission from the Food Allergy & Anaphylaxis Network,
2003*

**HOW TO READ A LABEL
for a TREE NUT-FREE DIET**
*Avoid foods that contain nuts or
any of these ingredients:*

almonds
artificial nuts
Brazil nuts
caponata
cashews
chestnuts
filbert/hazelnuts
gianduja (*a nut mixture found in
some chocolate*)
hickory nuts
macadamia nuts
mandelonas
marzipan/almond paste
nan-gai nuts
natural nut extract (*i.e., almond,
walnut*)
nougat
nut butters (*i.e., cashew butter*)
nut meal
nutmeat
nut oil

nut paste (*i.e., almond paste*)
nut pieces
pecans (*Mashuga Nuts®*)
pesto
pine nuts (*also referred to as
Indian, piñon, pinyon, pignoli,
pigñolia, and pignon nuts*)
pistachios
pralines
walnuts

• Mortadella may contain
pistachios.

• Natural and artificial flavoring
may contain tree nuts.

• Experts advise patients allergic
to tree nuts to avoid peanuts as
well.

• Talk to your doctor if you find
other nuts not listed here

*Printed with permission from the Food Allergy & Anaphylaxis Network,
2003*

HOW TO READ A LABEL for a GLUTEN-FREE DIET *Avoid foods that contain any of these ingredients:* wheat (see "How to read Label for Wheat-free Diet") barley (barley flour, barley malt, barley malt extract) rye oats triticale kamut spelt	May indicate presence of gluten: modified food starch unidentified food starch caramel coloring hydrolyzed plant protein (HPP) hydrolyzed vegetable protein (HVP) textured vegetable protein (TVP) mono- & di-glycerides (in dry products) malt, malt flavoring, or malt extract flavorings (natural and artificial) flavor extracts unidentified additives spice extracts brown rice syrup glucose syrup dextrin licorice soy sauce processed foods self-basting turkeys cold cuts prepared stocks and soups vinegars and alcohols

Reviewed by Celiac Sprue Association, 2003

COMMENTS

CHAPTER 12
RESOURCES

Support Organizations
Sources for Alternative Ingredients

SUPPORT ORGANIZATIONS

The following is a list of some resource organizations available for those with food allergies and celiac disease. Ask your healthcare provider about support groups in your local area. This list is not an endorsement of any organization.

Allergy & Asthma Network Mothers of Asthmatics (AANMA)
2751 Prosperity Ave., Suite 150, Fairfax, VA 22031
(800) 878-4403 / fax (703) 573-7794
www.aanma.org

American Academy of Allergy, Asthma & Immunology
611 East Wells Street, Milwaukee, WI 53202
(414) 272-6071 or (800) 822-2762
www.aaaai.org

American Celiac Society
PO Box 23455, New Orleans, LA 70183-0455
(504) 737-3293
AmerCeliacSoc@onebox.com

Celiac Sprue Association/USA
PO Box 31700, Omaha, NE 68131-0700
(402) 558-0600
www.csaceliacs.org

Food Allergy & Anaphylaxis Network (FAAN)
11781 Lee Jackson Memorial Hwy #160, Fairfax, VA 22033-3309
(800) 929-4040 / fax (703) 691-2713
www.foodallergy.org

Gluten Intolerance Group (GIG)
15110 10th Avenue SW, Suite A, Seattle, WA 98166-1820
(206) 246-6652 / fax (206) 246-6531
www.gluten.net

SOURCES FOR ALTERNATIVE INGREDIENTS

The following is a list of distributors of the alternative ingredients used in the recipes in this book. Your local health food store may carry many of the ingredients or can order them for you. You can also order directly from these companies.

Authentic Foods (bean flours, mixes)
1850 W. 169th Street, Suite B, Gardena, CA 90247
(800) 806-4737 or (310) 366-7612 / fax (310) 366-6938
www.authenticfoods.com

Bob's Red Mill Natural Foods, Inc. (flours, grains, baking aids)
5209 S. E. International Way, Milwaukie, Oregon 97222
(800) 349-2173 / fax (503) 653-1339
www.bobsredmill.com

Ener-G Foods, Inc. (Egg Replacer™, flours, mixes)
5960 First Avenue South, PO Box 84487
Seattle, WA 98124-5787
(800) 331-5222 / fax (206) 764-3398
www.ener-g.com

Gluten-Free Pantry (mixes, ingredients)
PO Box 840, Glastonbury, CT 06033
(800) 291-8386 or (806) 633-3826 / fax (806) 633-6853
www.glutenfree.com

Miss Roben's (flours, baked goods)
91 Western Maryland Parkway Suite 7
Hagerstown, MD 21740
(800) 891-0083 / (301) 631-5954 (fax)
www.missroben.com

Vermont Nut Free Chocolates (chocolates)
316 Route 2, PO Box 124, South Hero, VT 05486
(888) 468-8373 or (802) 372-4654
www.vermontnutfree.com

INDEX

Printed in the United States
32920LVS00002B/682-690